FAITH AND WISDOM – DEVOTIONAL FOR TEEN GIRLS

A 52-WEEK GUIDE TO DEEPEN FAITH, BUILD WISDOM, TRUST HIS PLAN, AND LIVE WITH GRACE THROUGH THE BIBLE AND PRAYER

DAVID & MARY BETH NELSON

CONTENTS

Stepping Forward   1

PART ONE
FAITH & IDENTITY IN CHRIST

Week 1   7
Faith in the Storm

Week 2   9
Who God Says You Are

Week 3   11
God's Plan vs. My Plan

Week 4   13
Faith Over Feelings

Week 5   15
Hearing God's Voice

Week 6   17
Overcoming Doubt

Week 7   19
Standing Firm in a Changing World

Week 8   21
Becoming a Woman of God

Week 9   23
The Armor of God

Week 10   25
The Power of Small Choices

Week 11   27
Living with Integrity

PART TWO
WISDOM, GROWTH & CHARACTER

Week 12   31
True Strength is Grace

Week 13   33
Bouncing Back from Mistakes

Week 14   35
Diligence & Hard Work

Week 15   37
Discipline Over Motivation

Week 16 39
Managing Emotions Wisely

Week 17 41
Overcoming Fear & Worry

Week 18 43
The Beauty of Patience

Week 19 45
Your Influence Matters

Week 20 47
Taking Responsibility

Week 21 49
Handling Criticism with Grace

Week 22 51
Breaking Free from Negative Patterns

PART THREE
FRIENDSHIPS, RELATIONSHIPS & SERVING OTHERS

Week 23 55
Choosing Friends Wisely

Week 24 57
Respecting Yourself & Others

Week 25 59
Dealing with Peer Pressure

Week 26 61
Finding Mentors & Role Models

Week 27 63
Resolving Conflict with Love

Week 28 65
A Heart Like His

Week 29 67
How to Apologize & Make Things Right

Week 30 69
Avoiding Gossip & Drama

Week 31 71
Dating with Wisdom and Worth

Week 32 73
The Strength to Say No

Week 33 75
Honoring Parents & Authority

Week 34 77
Navigating Family Relationships

Week 35   79
Encouraging & Lifting Others Up

Week 36   81
Leading by Example

PART FOUR
PURPOSE, GOALS & LIVING OUT FAITH

Week 37   85
Discovering Your Purpose

Week 38   87
Using Your Gifts & Talents

Week 39   89
Handling Disappointment with Grace

Week 40   91
Dreaming Big with God

Week 41   93
Why Effort Matters

Week 42   95
Money, Success & God's Perspective

Week 43   97
When Life Feels Unfair

Week 44   99
Dealing with Stress & Pressure

Week 45   101
What It Means to Lead

Week 46   103
Standing for What's Right

Week 47   105
Seeing the Least, Loving the Forgotten

Week 48   107
Choosing Kindness Daily

Week 49   109
Leaving a Legacy of Faith

Week 50   111
The Power of Gratitude

Week 51   113
Living with Intentionality

Week 52   115
Moving Forward in Faith

Moving Forward   117

STEPPING FORWARD

WELCOME TO *FAITH AND WISDOM*—A 52-week devotional designed to help you grow in your relationship with God, discover your identity, and walk through life with confidence, grace, and purpose. Each week, you'll dive into a powerful biblical truth that can shape how you think, speak, love, and lead—especially when it comes to showing kindness, standing strong, and trusting God's plan for your life.

This devotional isn't just about reading—it's about transformation. As you work through each weekly entry, you'll be invited to reflect deeply, live intentionally, and take simple, bold steps to apply your faith in your daily life. Whether you're facing friendship drama, school stress, self-doubt, or big dreams about your future—God's Word has wisdom for it all. And He's walking with you through every moment.

To help you get the most out of *Faith and Wisdom*, here's how each week is set up:

📖 Bible Verse

Each devotional begins with a Bible verse from the New International Version (NIV). This verse lays the foundation for the message. Take time to read it slowly—maybe even write it down or memorize it. Ask yourself: What is God saying to me through this?

✎ Devotional Message

This is where the verse comes to life. You'll read a short message that connects Scripture to your everyday experiences—whether it's friendships, choices, confidence, faith, or forgiveness. Read it thoughtfully, and try to picture how the message applies to your week ahead.

◡ Reflection Questions

After each message, you'll find three reflection questions to help you go deeper. These aren't for a grade—they're for you. Use them to journal, pray, or talk through with someone you trust. They'll help you explore what God is doing in your heart.

🚀 Challenge for the Week

Each devotional includes one simple, real-life challenge. It might be a way to show kindness, shift your perspective, pray differently, or step out in faith. These small steps can lead to big growth when you do them consistently.

🙏 Closing Prayer

Every week ends with a short prayer to help you connect with God and ask for His guidance. You can pray it once, or come back to it whenever you need strength or peace.

HOW TO BUILD A WEEKLY RHYTHM:

1️⃣ Pick a day to begin each devotional (many girls like Sundays or Mondays, but any day works).

2️⃣ Read the Bible verse and devotional. Highlight or underline anything that speaks to you.

3️⃣ Reflect on the questions—write them in a journal or talk them through with God.

4️⃣ Take action by starting your weekly challenge.

5️⃣ Pray the closing prayer and return to it anytime during the week.

6 Revisit the message midweek and ask: How is this shaping my thoughts, my heart, and my actions?

This journey isn't about being perfect—it's about becoming the young woman God created you to be. Some weeks will feel easy, and some will stretch you—but through it all, **you're growing in wisdom, strength, and faith**. Be patient with yourself, stay committed, and trust that God is doing His good work in you.

You are deeply loved, chosen with a purpose, and equipped for every good thing.

Let's begin this beautiful journey together. 🤍📖

PART ONE
FAITH & IDENTITY IN CHRIST

WEEK 1

FAITH IN THE STORM

START DATE: _____

Bible Verse: *"When you pass through the waters, I will be with you; and when you pass through the rivers, they will not sweep over you..."* — Isaiah 43:2 (NIV)

Devotional Message:

Life can feel overwhelming—friendships change, expectations pile up, and emotions run high. Maybe you're struggling with school stress, feeling left out, or facing personal challenges. In those moments, it's easy to feel like you're drowning, unsure if things will ever get better. But here's the truth: God is with you in every storm. He doesn't step away when life gets hard—He leans in closer.

Think of a lighthouse standing strong against crashing waves. No matter how fierce the storm, it doesn't move because it's built on a solid foundation. That's what God wants to be for you—your steady anchor. When the disciples were caught in a violent storm, Jesus calmed the sea with just His words (*Mark 4:39*). He may not always remove the storm immediately, but He promises peace in the middle of it.

Having faith in the storm doesn't mean ignoring your struggles. It means bringing your worries to God and trusting that He is stronger than your fears. *"My grace is sufficient for you, for my power is made perfect in weakness"* (2 Corinthians 12:9). You don't have to be the strongest person—God's strength is enough. And sometimes, strength looks like surrender—saying, "God, I need You."

Even Jesus faced storms—betrayal, rejection, and deep sorrow. But He never lost sight of God's presence. When life feels out of control, don't try to handle it alone. Pray, read Scripture, and remind yourself that God walks through every storm with you.

Maybe a friend is struggling, or you see someone being treated unfairly. It takes wisdom and courage to step in and offer support, but God calls you to be a light for others. He doesn't just help us through storms—He teaches us how to help others through theirs. Your comforted heart can become a source of comfort to someone else.

The storm may not end right away, but God's peace will sustain you. *"In this world you will have trouble. But take heart! I have overcome the world"* (John 16:33). No matter how uncertain things feel, you are never alone. You are held, loved, and strengthened by a God who speaks peace into every storm.

Reflection Questions:

1. What's a challenge in your life right now that feels overwhelming?
2. How can you remind yourself of God's presence when things feel out of control?
3. Who in your life might need encouragement in their own storm?

Challenge for the Week: Each morning, pray: *"God, help me trust You through every storm."* When you feel stressed, pause, take a deep breath, and remind yourself that God is your anchor.

Closing Prayer: *Lord, when life feels overwhelming, remind me that You are my refuge. Help me trust You, even when I can't see the way forward. Give me wisdom and courage to stand strong and to encourage others who are struggling. Thank You for walking with me through every storm. Amen.*

WEEK 2
WHO GOD SAYS YOU ARE

START DATE: _____

Bible Verse: *"You are altogether beautiful, my darling; there is no flaw in you."* — Song of Solomon 4:7 (NIV)

Devotional Message:

Who are you? The world tries to define you by your looks, popularity, achievements, or how many likes you get on social media. Maybe you feel like you don't measure up—like you're not pretty enough, smart enough, or good enough.

But here's the truth: Your worth isn't based on what the world says —it's based on what God says.

And what does God say? He calls you His daughter, loved and chosen (*1 Peter 2:9*). He says you are fearfully and wonderfully made (*Psalm 139:14*). He says you are valuable—not because of what you do, but because of who you are in Him. His voice speaks truth that cuts through all the noise around you.

Think about a $100 bill. If it gets crumpled, stepped on, or stained, does it lose its value? No. It's still worth the same. In the same way, your worth doesn't decrease because of mistakes, failures, or what others think of you.

God created you with intention, and nothing can change that.

When Jesus walked on Earth, He spent time with people the world overlooked—tax collectors, outcasts, and sinners. He didn't see them for their past or their status; He saw their hearts. And He sees you the same way.

No matter how you feel about yourself, God sees you as His masterpiece (*Ephesians 2:10*).

But the enemy wants you to believe otherwise. Satan whispers lies that you're not enough, that you need to change to be accepted. But *John 8:44* reminds us that the devil is the father of lies—his goal is to make you doubt your identity in Christ. That's why it's so important to fill your heart with God's truth.

The next time insecurity creeps in, remind yourself: I am loved. I am chosen. I am enough in Christ.

God doesn't make mistakes, and He didn't make one when He created you. The more you focus on what He says, the less power the world's opinions will have over you.

Reflection Questions:

1. When do you feel most insecure? What triggers those feelings?
2. What is one Bible verse you can hold onto when you doubt your worth?
3. How can you remind yourself daily that your identity is in Christ, not in others' opinions?

Challenge for the Week: Each morning, look in the mirror and say: *"I am God's masterpiece. He created me with purpose."* Write down three things you love about yourself—not just your appearance, but who you are inside.

Closing Prayer: *Lord, remind me that my worth is found in You, not in the opinions of others. Help me to see myself the way You see me—loved, chosen, and valuable. Silence the lies that tell me I'm not enough, and fill my heart with Your truth. Thank You for creating me with purpose. Amen.*

WEEK 3

GOD'S PLAN VS. MY PLAN

START DATE: _____

Bible Verse: *"'For I know the plans I have for you,' declares the Lord, 'plans to prosper you and not to harm you, plans to give you hope and a future.'"* — Jeremiah 29:11 (NIV)

Devotional Message:

Have you ever had your heart set on something—making a team, getting into a certain school, or having a relationship work out— only for things to go differently than you planned?

It's frustrating when life doesn't go the way we expect, and it's easy to wonder, *Does God really know what He's doing?*

The truth is, God sees the bigger picture. While we focus on what's right in front of us, He sees where we're headed and what's truly best for us.

Proverbs 3:5-6 says, *"Trust in the Lord with all your heart and lean not on your own understanding; in all your ways submit to him, and he will make your paths straight."*

Think of a GPS. You might think you know the best route, but sometimes it recalculates because there's traffic or a roadblock ahead. God does the same with our lives. He redirects us—not to ruin our plans, but to protect us from something we can't see or to guide us toward something even better.

It's hard to surrender when we want things *our* way. But look at Jesus. Before His crucifixion, He prayed, *"Father, if you are willing, take this cup from me; yet not my will, but yours be done"* (Luke 22:42).

Jesus, though perfect, still surrendered to God's plan—even when it was painful—because He trusted that God's plan was greater.

The same applies to us. We might experience disappointment or confusion, but God is always working behind the scenes. What feels like a "no" now might be making way for a better "yes" later. The key is trusting Him even when we don't understand.

So, when life doesn't go your way, don't let frustration turn into doubt. Instead, ask, *God, what are You teaching me? What better plan do You have?*

When you shift your focus from "Why is this happening?" to "How can I trust God in this?", your faith will grow stronger.

Reflection Questions:

1. Have you ever had something not go as planned but later realized it was for the best?
2. What is one area of your life where you struggle to trust God's plan?
3. How can you remind yourself that God sees the bigger picture?

Challenge for the Week: Each morning, pray: *"God, I trust Your plan for my life, even when I don't understand it."* If something doesn't go your way this week, pause and ask, *What might God be doing through this?*

Closing Prayer: *Lord, help me to trust Your plan, even when it's different from mine. I know You see what I cannot. Give me patience, wisdom, and faith to surrender my desires to You. Remind me that Your plans are always for my good. Amen.*

WEEK 4

FAITH OVER FEELINGS

START DATE: _____

Bible Verse: *"The heart is deceitful above all things and beyond cure. Who can understand it?"* — Jeremiah 17:9 (NIV)

Devotional Message:

Feelings can be powerful. One moment, you're excited and confident; the next, you're discouraged and anxious. Maybe you've felt unworthy because of a bad day or doubted yourself because of what someone said. But here's the truth: your feelings don't define you—God does.

The world tells us, *"Follow your heart,"* but the Bible warns that our hearts can be deceiving (Jeremiah 17:9). Feelings are real, but they aren't always reliable. One day, you might feel close to God; the next, you might feel distant. But God hasn't changed—only your emotions have. That's why it's important to build your life on faith, not feelings.

Think about a cloudy day. Just because you can't see the sun doesn't mean it's not there. In the same way, just because you don't *feel* God's presence doesn't mean He isn't with you. Hebrews 13:5 reminds us, *"Never will I leave you; never will I forsake you."*

Jesus understands emotions—He felt sadness, joy, exhaustion, and even fear. Before His crucifixion, He prayed, *"My soul is overwhelmed with sorrow to the point of death"* (Matthew 26:38). Yet, instead of letting fear lead Him, He chose faith: *"Not my will, but yours be done"* (Luke 22:42).

So how do we put faith above feelings? First, anchor yourself in truth. When insecurity creeps in, remind yourself of what God says: *You are loved. You are chosen. You are enough in Christ.* Second, pray through your emotions. Tell God how you feel, but don't let those feelings control your choices. Finally, take action in faith. Even when you don't *feel* like worshiping, reading your Bible, or praying—do it anyway.

Faith grows when you trust God, not just when you feel close to Him.

Life will have ups and downs, but God remains constant. Your emotions will shift, but His truth never does.

When you feel overwhelmed, ask yourself: *Am I being led by my feelings or by my faith?* Let faith be your guide.

Reflection Questions:

1. When have your emotions led you to believe something that wasn't true?
2. What Bible verse can you hold onto when your feelings try to control you?
3. How can you practice choosing faith over feelings this week?

Challenge for the Week: Each morning, pray: *"God, help me trust Your truth over my emotions today."* When you feel overwhelmed, pause and remind yourself: Feelings change, but God stays the same.

Closing Prayer: *Lord, help me not to be led by my emotions, but by faith in You. When I feel anxious, remind me of Your truth. When I feel discouraged, strengthen my heart. Teach me to trust You, even when I don't feel it. Amen.*

WEEK 5

HEARING GOD'S VOICE

START DATE: _____

Bible Verse: *"My sheep listen to my voice; I know them, and they follow me."* — John 10:27 (NIV)

Devotional Message:

Have you ever wished God would just text you or write His answer in the sky? You're not alone. Many people—teens and adults alike—wonder how to know if it's really God speaking or just their own thoughts. You might pray and still ask, *Was that You, God? Or was that just me hoping for an answer?*

The good news? God is always speaking—we just have to learn how to listen. This week's verse says that if you belong to Him, you can hear Him. It may take time, but as your relationship with Him grows, His voice becomes easier to recognize.

God speaks in different ways, and each one helps us know Him better. He speaks through the Bible, which is the clearest way to hear His voice. When you read it, ask God to help you understand it. His Word can guide your next step—even when the future feels foggy.

He also speaks through prayer. Prayer isn't just about talking—it's also about listening. Try sitting in silence after you pray. You may not hear words, but sometimes a new idea, a moment of peace, or clarity rises—and you just know it didn't come from you.

The Holy Spirit speaks too. That quiet conviction about a choice, the peace you feel after praying, or a strong sense of "this is right"—those are often His nudges. He helps guide, comfort, and remind you of what's true.

God also speaks through wise people in your life—like mentors, parents, or friends who follow Him. *Proverbs 11:14* says, *"Victory is won through many advisers."* If someone says something that lines up with Scripture and brings peace, it could be God using them to speak to you.

If you feel like you're not hearing anything, don't get discouraged. God may already be speaking in ways you haven't noticed yet. His voice isn't always loud—but it is always full of love. Trust takes time. The more you spend with Him, the more you'll know His voice—just like you recognize your best friend's voice in a crowd.

And the more you hear Him, the more confident you'll become in following where He leads.

Reflection Questions:

1. Have you ever felt God speaking to you? What happened?
2. Which of the four ways God speaks do you need to grow in?
3. How can you create more space to hear from God this week?

Challenge for the Week: Each day, set aside five minutes of quiet time. Read a short passage from Psalms or Proverbs, then sit in stillness and pray, "God, what do You want to show me today?"

Closing Prayer: *Lord, teach me to recognize Your voice. Help me to slow down and listen—not just with my ears, but with my heart. Speak through Your Word, through prayer, and through the people You've placed in my life. Guide me to follow You with confidence and peace. Amen.*

WEEK 6

OVERCOMING DOUBT

START DATE: _____

Bible Verse: *"Immediately Jesus reached out his hand and caught him. 'You of little faith,' he said, 'why did you doubt?'"* — Matthew 14:31 (NIV)

Devotional Message:

Everyone struggles with doubt.

Maybe you wonder if God is really listening, if He has a plan for you, or if your faith is strong enough. Doubt doesn't mean you've failed—it's part of growing. Even some of the greatest people in the Bible wrestled with it.

Peter did. One night, when Jesus walked on water, Peter stepped out of the boat to join Him. At first, he walked on the waves. But when he saw the wind and waves, he panicked and began sinking. Jesus reached out and caught him—and that's when He said, *"You of little faith, why did you doubt?"* (Matthew 14:31).

Peter's mistake wasn't stepping out in faith—it was taking his eyes off Jesus. When he focused on the storm instead of the Savior, doubt took over. The same happens to us. When we focus on our fears, insecurities, or the opinions of others, our faith can feel shaky. But just like Jesus caught Peter, He's always there to catch you. He doesn't wait for perfect faith—He responds to even the smallest step toward Him. Doubt isn't the opposite of faith—it's an opportunity to strengthen it.

Instead of running from questions, bring them to God. He isn't afraid of your doubts. In *Mark 9:24*, a man cried out to Jesus, *"I do believe; help me overcome my unbelief!"* Jesus didn't reject him—He helped him. He still helps us today.

So how do you overcome doubt? First, focus on what you know. When uncertainty creeps in, remind yourself of God's past faithfulness. Second, stay rooted in His Word. *Romans 10:17* says, *"Faith comes from hearing the message, and the message is heard through the word about Christ."* The more you fill your heart with truth, the stronger your faith will grow.

Finally, choose faith, even when you don't feel it. Faith isn't about having zero doubts—it's about trusting God despite them. It's about looking to Him when everything else feels uncertain.

If you wait until every question is answered, you'll never step out of the boat. But when you do, you'll find that God is there, reaching out His hand to steady you—and walking beside you through every wave.

Reflection Questions:

1. What doubts have you struggled with about your faith?
2. How can you remind yourself of God's faithfulness when you feel uncertain?
3. What step of faith can you take this week, even if doubt is present?

Challenge for the Week: Write down one past moment when you saw God's faithfulness. When doubt creeps in, reread it and remind yourself that God is still with you.

Closing Prayer: *Lord, I know doubt is part of my journey, but I don't want it to control me. Help me trust You, even when I don't understand everything. Strengthen my faith and remind me of Your presence. Thank You for always being there to catch me. Amen.*

WEEK 7

STANDING FIRM IN A CHANGING WORLD

START DATE: _____

Bible Verse: *"Do not conform to the pattern of this world, but be transformed by the renewing of your mind."* — Romans 12:2 (NIV)

Devotional Message:

Culture changes fast. One day a trend is everywhere, and the next it's forgotten. Social media opinions shift daily, and it can feel like you're always trying to keep up. But deep down, you know that chasing approval and fitting in can be exhausting—and even empty. That's because the world's pattern doesn't match God's design for you.

God doesn't call you to blend in—He calls you to stand out. While the world encourages you to follow whatever feels good, God invites you to live by something deeper: truth, integrity, and faith. When you follow Him, your life begins to look different from the crowd—and that's a good thing. It's not about being perfect, but about being faithful to who God made you to be.

Imagine a tree planted beside a stream, its roots going deep into the soil. No matter what storms come, the tree stays standing because it's anchored. That's how your faith works when your mind is being renewed by God's Word. The more time you spend with Him, the stronger your roots grow, and the less likely you are to be shaken by pressure or popularity.

Even Jesus faced pressure to conform. When He was tempted by Satan in the wilderness, He was offered power, comfort, and recognition. But He stood firm, answering each temptation with Scripture. He didn't waver, and His strength came from knowing the truth (*Matthew 4:1–11*). You have access to that same truth today.

So how do you stand strong when everything around you is pushing a different direction? First, get grounded in what you believe. That means regularly reading Scripture, even when you don't feel like it. Let God's truth shape how you think, what you value, and how you respond. Second, choose your community wisely. Friends who follow Christ can support you when it feels hard to stand alone. And third, stay connected to God in prayer. Ask for courage, wisdom, and clarity. He promises to guide you.

You were never meant to be a copy of the world. You were created to reflect something far greater—God's image. When you live that out, you become a light in a culture that's constantly shifting. Others may notice, ask questions, or even be inspired to stand firm too. And through it all, God will be your steady guide.

Reflection Questions:

1. When have you felt pressure to conform to the world's standards?
2. What are some Bible verses you can hold onto when you need strength to stand firm?
3. How can you encourage others to stay strong in their faith?

Challenge for the Week: Choose one area where you've felt pressure to compromise and pray about it each day. Ask God to help you stand firm and stay true to who He's called you to be.

Closing Prayer: *Lord, the world is always changing, but You remain the same. Help me stand firm in my faith, even when I feel pressured to compromise. Give me wisdom to recognize what is true and the courage to live it out. Thank You for being my unshakable foundation. Amen.*

WEEK 8

BECOMING A WOMAN OF GOD

START DATE: _____

Bible Verse: *"Charm is deceptive, and beauty is fleeting; but a woman who fears the Lord is to be praised."* — Proverbs 31:30 (NIV)

Devotional Message:

What does it mean to be a woman of God? The world often defines womanhood by appearance, popularity, or success. Social media is filled with messages telling you how to look, act, or think to be accepted. But God's definition is different—He values a heart that seeks Him above all else.

Proverbs 31:30 reminds us that charm can be misleading and beauty fades over time. This verse isn't saying beauty or personality are bad things, but they're not the foundation of lasting worth. True beauty isn't found in a flawless appearance or a perfect life—it's found in a heart that honors God. What God sees as praiseworthy isn't what the world praises—it's a life rooted in reverence, trust, and love for Him. And when your heart is anchored in God, it shines with a beauty that doesn't fade.

Throughout the Bible, strong women of faith stood out—not for their looks or status, but for their trust in God and their willingness to follow Him. Esther was brave enough to risk her life to save her people (*Esther 4:16*). Ruth remained faithful and loyal, even when her future was uncertain (*Ruth 1:16–17*). Mary, the mother of Jesus, said yes to God's plan despite her fear and the unknown (*Luke 1:38*). These women weren't perfect, but their faith made them bold and beautiful in God's eyes.

So how do you grow into a woman of God? First, prioritize your relationship with Him. Spending time in prayer and Scripture helps you hear His voice and understand His will for your life. Second, focus on godly character. A woman of God is compassionate, wise, and courageous—not because she has it all together, but because she relies on God's strength when she doesn't. Third, live with purpose. God created you with unique gifts and passions, and He invites you to use them to serve others and glorify Him.

Being a woman of God doesn't mean being perfect. It means choosing to follow Him daily, standing firm in faith, and showing love in a world that desperately needs it.

The world may try to define you by your image or achievements, but God already has.

You are His daughter—created with intention, called with purpose, and deeply loved.

Reflection Questions:

1. What qualities do you think define a woman of God?
2. How can you focus more on inner character rather than outward appearance?
3. What steps can you take to grow into the woman God created you to be?

Challenge for the Week: Write down three qualities of a woman of God you want to develop. Pray about them daily, asking God to shape your heart and character.

Closing Prayer: *Lord, help me become the woman You created me to be. Teach me to value what You value and to find my worth in You, not the world. Strengthen my faith, shape my character, and guide me in Your wisdom. When I feel pressured to measure up to the world's standards, remind me that my identity is in You alone. Amen.*

WEEK 9
THE ARMOR OF GOD

START DATE: _____

Bible Verse: *"Put on the full armor of God, so that you can take your stand against the devil's schemes."* — Ephesians 6:11 (NIV)

Devotional Message:

Life is full of battles—temptations, doubts, pressures, and struggles.

Some days, it might feel like everything is working against you: school stress, friendship drama, family tension, or even negative thoughts you can't seem to shake. The enemy wants to distract you, discourage you, and make you forget who you are.

But the good news is that God has already equipped you with what you need to stand strong.

He gives you spiritual armor—tools to protect your heart, your mind, and your faith. Each part of the armor has a purpose and strengthens you in a different way. And this armor isn't just symbolic—it's powerful and practical for your everyday life.

The Belt of Truth helps you stay grounded when the world tries to confuse you (*Ephesians 6:14*). When you know what's true, lies lose their power. The Breastplate of Righteousness protects your heart when you choose to live with integrity and follow God's ways (*Ephesians 6:14*). The Shoes of Peace, described as readiness from the gospel, help you walk with calm confidence, no matter what chaos is around you (*Ephesians 6:15*).

The Shield of Faith guards you from fear, doubt, and discouragement—it reminds you that God is bigger than your battles (*Ephesians 6:16*). The Helmet of Salvation covers your thoughts and reminds you who you belong to—saved, loved, and chosen (*Ephesians 6:17*). And the Sword of the Spirit, which is the Word of God, is your weapon. When you feel attacked by lies, Scripture helps you fight back with truth (*Ephesians 6:17*).

Putting on this armor doesn't happen automatically. It's a daily choice to invite God into your life, lean on His Word, and trust Him to prepare you for whatever comes your way. The more you make that a habit, the more confident and secure you'll feel—even in difficult moments.

You don't have to fight every battle alone.

When you wear God's armor, you walk in His strength, not just your own. That changes everything. And with His power at work in you, even the hardest battles can become victories.

Reflection Questions:

1. Which piece of the armor of God do you need to strengthen in your life?
2. How can you use God's Word as a weapon against doubt and temptation?
3. What practical steps can you take to remind yourself to "put on" the armor of God each day?

Challenge for the Week: Each morning, take one minute to pray through each piece of armor. Ask God to protect your mind, guide your actions, and strengthen your faith. Memorize Ephesians 6:11 as a daily reminder that you are equipped.

Closing Prayer: *Lord, thank You for giving me the armor I need to stand strong. Help me to put on Your truth, righteousness, peace, faith, salvation, and Word daily. Protect my heart and mind from doubt and temptation. Strengthen me to live boldly for You. Amen.*

WEEK 10

THE POWER OF SMALL CHOICES

START DATE: _____

Bible Verse: *"Whoever can be trusted with very little can also be trusted with much."* — Luke 16:10 (NIV)

Devotional Message:

Every choice you make—big or small—shapes your future. It's easy to think the little things don't matter: whether you respond with kindness, whether you're honest about something small, or whether you take time to pray. But in God's eyes, the little things reveal what's really going on in your heart.

Think of a trail in the woods. Each small step may seem insignificant, but over time, those steps determine where you end up. The way you speak, the way you spend your time, and the habits you build—they're all leading somewhere. Are they drawing you closer to God or pulling you away?

God sees the small things as training ground. If you can be trusted with a little—like keeping your word or doing what's right when no one's watching—you're being prepared for more. Growth happens through small, faithful choices. Even when no one else notices, God sees your obedience and honors it. Faithfulness in the small things is how trust, strength, and character are formed.

Think about David. Before he was king, he was a shepherd—an ordinary job. But he protected the sheep and relied on God. When he faced Goliath, he was ready. His courage came from years of quiet obedience. (See *1 Samuel 17*.) The small things prepared him for the big moment, even if he didn't realize it at the time.

The enemy wants you to believe that skipping prayer or telling a small lie doesn't matter. But small compromises add up. They shape how you think and who you're becoming. On the other hand, faithful choices build strength and draw you closer to God. You're not just building habits—you're building a foundation.

So how do you make wise choices? First, ask, "Does this honor God?" If it doesn't, choose something better. Second, build habits that grow your faith. Reading Scripture, showing kindness, or forgiving may feel small, but they have lasting impact. And finally, trust that even when no one notices, God does.

One small step in the right direction can lead to something greater. Don't underestimate what God can do through your quiet yes. The life He's building in you often starts with one faithful decision at a time.

Reflection Questions:

1. What small habits are shaping your faith—for better or worse?
2. Have you ever seen how a small decision had a big impact on your life?
3. What small step can you take this week to grow closer to God?

Challenge for the Week: Choose one small habit to improve— prayer, kindness, honesty, or something else. Be intentional about it every day and notice how it strengthens your faith by the end of the week.

Closing Prayer: *Lord, help me to see that even my smallest choices matter. Teach me to be faithful in the little things so I can grow into the person You've called me to be. Give me wisdom to make decisions that honor You. Amen.*

WEEK 11
LIVING WITH INTEGRITY

START DATE: _____

Bible Verse: *"The integrity of the upright guides them, but the unfaithful are destroyed by their duplicity."* — Proverbs 11:3 (NIV)

Devotional Message:

Integrity means doing what's right even when no one is watching. It's easy to be honest when people are paying attention, but real integrity is about who you are *all the time*—not just when others see. It's being consistent in your words, actions, and values.

Duplicity is the opposite—it means saying one thing and doing another, pretending to be someone you're not. That kind of living eventually catches up with you. It leads to broken trust, guilt, and confusion. But when you walk in integrity, you live with clarity, peace, and a steady heart, even when life gets hard.

Joseph in the Bible is a powerful example. After being sold into slavery, he worked in Potiphar's house and was tempted to sin. No one would have known if he gave in. But Joseph refused, saying, "How then could I do such a wicked thing and sin against God?" (Genesis 39:9). His decision cost him his freedom, but it protected his character and honored God.

You'll face moments like that too—not always dramatic, but still defining. Maybe it's the choice to be honest about something you did wrong. Maybe it's not laughing at a cruel joke, not joining in gossip, or not pretending to be someone you're not just to fit in. Every small choice builds a stronger foundation.

Think of integrity like a house built on solid rock. It may take time to build, and it won't always look flashy—but it lasts. When life gets shaky, your foundation holds.

That's what integrity does. It guides you when you're unsure. It strengthens you when you're tempted. And it keeps your heart aligned with God's.

So how do you grow in integrity? First, commit to telling the truth, even in small things. Second, be consistent—don't have one personality for school and another for church. Third, pray for courage. God will help you do the right thing, even when it's hard.

Integrity doesn't guarantee an easy life, but it leads to a meaningful one. People will trust you, and more importantly, your relationship with God will be built on honesty and strength.

Reflection Questions:

1. When have you faced a situation where it was hard to be honest?
2. What small habits can you practice to build a life of integrity?
3. How can you remind yourself to choose honesty, even when it's difficult?

Challenge for the Week: Before making a decision, ask yourself: "Would I still do this if everyone knew— including God?" Choose honesty and integrity in small things, and they will become part of your character.

Closing Prayer: *Lord, help me be a person of integrity. Give me the strength to choose honesty, even when it's hard. Let my actions reflect my faith, and remind me that who I am when no one is watching matters to You. Amen.*

PART TWO
WISDOM, GROWTH & CHARACTER

WEEK 12

TRUE STRENGTH IS GRACE

START DATE: _____

Bible Verse: *"My grace is sufficient for you, for my power is made perfect in weakness."* — 2 Corinthians 12:9 (NIV)

Devotional Message:

The world often teaches that strength means being tough, never showing weakness, and always proving yourself. But God's definition of strength is different. He doesn't expect perfection—He invites dependence. Real strength is found in grace.

God's power shows up best not when we have it all together, but when we admit we don't. When we stop pretending to be strong on our own, we make room for His strength to carry us. Grace fills the gaps where our strength runs out. It reminds us that we are not alone, even when we feel overwhelmed or inadequate. God's strength isn't loud or showy—it's steady, present, and full of peace.

Look at Jesus. He had the power to silence His enemies, but He chose a path of grace. When He was arrested and beaten, He didn't fight back. On the cross, He prayed for the very people who crucified Him, saying, *"Father, forgive them, for they do not know what they are doing"* (*Luke 23:34*). The world might have seen weakness, but He showed the strongest kind of love.

Grace isn't weakness. It's choosing kindness when someone is rude. It's forgiving instead of holding a grudge. It's walking away from an argument when you could easily win it. Grace takes more strength than revenge ever will. It's not about being passive—it's about being powered by something deeper than pride.

Think about a time when someone hurt you. Maybe they embarrassed you, excluded you, or betrayed your trust. The easy thing might be to stay mad, but grace offers freedom—for you and for them. When you forgive, you're not saying what they did was okay; you're choosing to trust God with the outcome. Forgiveness isn't letting someone off the hook—it's releasing your own heart from the weight of bitterness.

So how do you live with grace? First, accept it. You don't have to earn God's love. He gives it freely—even when you mess up. Second, extend it. Look for chances to respond with patience instead of irritation. And third, rely on God when you feel weak. You don't have to carry everything on your own. He will give you the strength you need.

When you walk in grace, you walk in God's power. That's real strength. And when you lead with grace, others see a glimpse of the love and power of Jesus in you.

Reflection Questions:

1. When have you seen grace in action—either in your life or in someone else's?
2. Why do you think it takes strength to show grace?
3. How can you rely on God's grace in your daily struggles?

Challenge for the Week: When faced with frustration, pause and choose grace. Instead of reacting in anger, respond with kindness. Pray for the people who challenge you the most.

Closing Prayer: *Lord, thank You for Your grace. I know I don't have to be perfect because Your strength fills my weaknesses. Help me to show grace to others, even when it's hard. Teach me to rely on You instead of trying to do everything on my own. Amen.*

WEEK 13

BOUNCING BACK FROM MISTAKES

START DATE: _____

Bible Verse: *"Though the righteous fall seven times, they rise again, but the wicked stumble when calamity strikes."* — Proverbs 24:16 (NIV)

Devotional Message:

Everyone makes mistakes. Maybe you said something you regret, hurt a friend, or made a bad decision. When we mess up, it's easy to feel ashamed or believe we've failed God. But falling short doesn't mean it's over. With God, there's always a chance to begin again.

Even people who love God stumble. The difference is, they get back up. That's what real faith looks like—not perfection, but persistence. God isn't expecting you to have it all together. He's simply asking you to keep turning to Him, no matter how many times you fall. Every time you return to Him, He meets you with open arms—not disappointment, but love.

Think about Peter. He had walked closely with Jesus, but when pressure hit, he denied even knowing Him—not once, but three times (*Luke 22:61–62*). He must have felt crushed by guilt. But Jesus didn't reject him. After rising from the dead, He met Peter with grace and restoration (*John 21:15–17*). That failure didn't end Peter's story—it became part of how God used him to lead others.

When you make a mistake, start by being honest. Don't cover it up or pretend it didn't happen. Confess it to God and ask for forgiveness. According to *1 John 1:9*, when we confess, God is faithful and just to forgive us. Then take a step forward. Mistakes can become growth moments if you're willing to learn from them.

There may be voices—external or internal—that try to convince you you're not good enough, that you'll never change, or that it's too late. Don't believe them. Those thoughts don't come from God. His voice calls you back with grace and hope, not shame.

It's also important to forgive yourself. Sometimes that's the hardest part. But if God—who is perfect—has chosen to forgive you, then you can choose to let go of guilt too. Holding on only keeps you stuck. Walking in freedom means accepting God's mercy and choosing to believe your future is still full of purpose.

No matter how many times you've fallen, God's love is steady. He's not done with you. He lifts you up, again and again, and gently reminds you: this isn't the end of your story.

It's the beginning of a comeback built on grace.

Reflection Questions:

1. Have you ever made a mistake that felt impossible to recover from? How did God bring you through it?
2. Why do you think it's easier to show grace to others than to yourself?
3. How can you remind yourself of God's forgiveness when you feel like you've failed?

Challenge for the Week: If you're holding onto guilt over a past mistake, bring it to God. Pray, confess, and ask for His forgiveness. Then let it go, trusting that He already has.

Closing Prayer: *Lord, thank You for Your grace that lifts me when I fall. Help me to learn from my mistakes instead of letting them define me. Teach me to accept Your forgiveness and extend that same grace to myself and others. Thank You for always giving me a fresh start. Amen.*

WEEK 14
DILIGENCE & HARD WORK

START DATE: _____

Bible Verse: *"Whatever you do, work at it with all your heart, as working for the Lord, not for human masters."* — Colossians 3:23 (NIV)

Devotional Message:

Have you ever been tempted to give less than your best—maybe rushing through homework, skipping chores, or doing just enough to get by? It's easy to fall into the mindset of "no one's going to notice," especially when the task seems boring or unimportant. But God notices. And He cares about your effort, not just your results.

When you work with your whole heart, you're not just checking off a to-do list—you're growing in character. Diligence teaches discipline, faithfulness, and perseverance. These are the habits that help shape who you're becoming—not just as a student, friend, or family member, but as a follower of Christ. A strong work ethic isn't just about productivity—it's a reflection of your values and your heart. And over time, those small daily choices can build a legacy of trustworthiness and strength.

One powerful example of this kind of dedication comes from Nehemiah. He led the rebuilding of Jerusalem's wall, a huge and difficult task. It was tiring, and not everyone supported him. Some even tried to distract and discourage him. But Nehemiah stayed focused, saying, *"I am doing a great work and I cannot come down"* (*Nehemiah 6:3*). He understood that his work mattered—not because it was easy or glamorous, but because it honored God.

Diligence doesn't mean perfection or overworking yourself. Even God rested after creating the world (*Genesis 2:2*). True diligence is about showing up with purpose, giving your best, and trusting God with the results. It's about doing small things with a big heart. God doesn't overlook the effort you put in behind the scenes—He uses it to shape your future.

So how can you build diligence in your everyday life? First, change your perspective. Instead of dreading the task, ask how you can honor God through it. Second, stick with it—even when it's hard or unnoticed. Faithfulness in small things prepares you for bigger ones. And third, ask God for strength when you feel tired, distracted, or discouraged. He will help you stay focused.

Whether it's cleaning your room, finishing an assignment, or helping a sibling, your attitude matters. When you give your best with the right heart, it becomes more than a task—it becomes worship. And that kind of heart honors God in everything you do.

Reflection Questions:

1. What task or responsibility do you struggle to give your best effort in?
2. How can you shift your mindset to see work as an opportunity to honor God?
3. What is one small step you can take to be more diligent this week?

Challenge for the Week: Pick one daily task—something simple— and choose to do it with excellence all week long. Treat it as if you're doing it directly for God, and notice how your attitude changes.

Closing Prayer: *Lord, help me to work with diligence and excellence, not for recognition, but to honor You. Give me perseverance when I feel unmotivated and remind me that my efforts matter. Teach me to balance hard work with rest and to trust You with the results. Amen.*

WEEK 15

DISCIPLINE OVER MOTIVATION

START DATE: _____

Bible Verse: *"No discipline seems pleasant at the time, but painful. Later on, however, it produces a harvest of righteousness and peace for those who have been trained by it."* — Hebrews 12:11 (NIV)

Devotional Message:

Some days, you wake up feeling motivated and ready to tackle your goals. Other days, even simple tasks feel like a struggle. If you rely only on motivation, you'll find it hard to stay consistent. That's why discipline matters so much more—because it keeps you going when motivation fades.

Discipline isn't always exciting. It means doing the right thing, even when you don't feel like it. But over time, that consistency leads to real growth. Whether it's building your faith, doing well in school, showing kindness, or sticking with your responsibilities, discipline strengthens your character and deepens your relationship with God.

Think about an athlete preparing for a race. They don't train only when they're in the mood—they show up every day, knowing that hard work adds up. The same is true in your spiritual life. You grow when you choose to pray, read the Bible, and follow God—not just when it's easy, but especially when it's hard.

The strongest faith is built in the quiet, unseen moments of daily perseverance. That kind of consistency honors God far more than bursts of short-lived motivation.

Jesus gave us the ultimate example of discipline. Before the cross, He prayed in deep sorrow, asking if there was another way. But He surrendered to God's will and followed through, even though it meant great suffering (Luke 22:42). That's not a story about motivation—it's about love, obedience, and deep commitment.

So how do you build that kind of discipline? It begins with small, intentional choices—like committing to a daily prayer time or setting aside a few quiet minutes for Scripture. When you face resistance or distractions, remind yourself why it matters. Discipline grows when you press forward through discomfort and stay steady when it would be easier to give up. You don't have to rely on your own strength, either. God is with you, ready to give you endurance, focus, and peace as you stay faithful in the little things.

Discipline doesn't mean you won't stumble. It means you keep going even after you do. When you stay committed, even imperfectly, God uses your efforts to shape your heart.

One small step at a time, you're becoming stronger, more focused, and more faithful.

Reflection Questions:

1. In what area of your life do you struggle to stay disciplined?
2. How can you push through when motivation is low?
3. What daily habit can you start to help strengthen your discipline?

Challenge for the Week: Pick one habit—prayer, Bible reading, schoolwork, or fitness—and commit to doing it daily, even when you don't feel like it.

Closing Prayer: *Lord, help me to develop discipline in my life. When I don't feel motivated, give me the strength to stay committed. Teach me to trust You and to push through challenges, knowing that You are shaping me into the person You've called me to be. Amen.*

WEEK 16
MANAGING EMOTIONS WISELY

START DATE: _____

Bible Verse: *"Fools give full vent to their rage, but the wise bring calm in the end."* — Proverbs 29:11 (NIV)

Devotional Message:

Emotions are a natural part of life. Some days you feel joyful and confident. Other days, anger, sadness, or anxiety seem to take over. God created emotions, but He doesn't want them to control us. Instead, He invites us to handle them with wisdom, patience, and grace.

When emotions run high, it's easy to react in the moment—snapping in frustration, shutting down in sadness, or making impulsive choices out of fear. But quick reactions often lead to words or actions we later regret. Emotions are real, but they aren't always right. Learning to pause gives space for reflection—and gives God room to speak into the moment.

Even Jesus felt deep emotions. He wept when His friend Lazarus died (*John 11:35*). He showed righteous anger when He saw injustice in the temple (*Matthew 21:12–13*). He experienced overwhelming sorrow before going to the cross (*Matthew 26:38*). Yet in every situation, He responded with purpose and composure, honoring God in how He handled each feeling.

39

Learning to manage emotions wisely is part of growing in maturity and faith. When you're upset or overwhelmed, take a moment to pause before reacting. That pause is powerful—it gives you a chance to breathe, think, and invite God into the moment. Talking to Him about what you're feeling is one of the healthiest things you can do. He offers peace when your emotions feel like too much. You don't have to have all the answers—you just need to turn to the One who does.

It also helps to filter what you're feeling through God's truth. You might feel like no one cares, but Scripture reminds you that you're deeply loved and never alone. You might feel like you're failing, but God says His strength is made perfect in your weakness. When emotions speak loudly, let God's Word speak louder.

Self-control doesn't mean pretending you don't feel things. It means choosing how you respond, even in the middle of strong emotion. That's where wisdom grows. That's where peace begins. And that's where you start to reflect God's character—even in tough moments.

God doesn't expect perfection, but He does invite you to grow. With His help, you can learn to respond with calm instead of chaos, grace instead of outbursts, and wisdom instead of impulse. And the more you practice it, the more natural it becomes to turn to Him first.

Reflection Questions:

1. How do you usually handle strong emotions?
2. What is one emotion that tends to control your actions?
3. How can you practice responding with wisdom instead of reacting impulsively?

Challenge for the Week: When you feel a strong emotion—anger, sadness, or fear—pause before reacting. Take a deep breath, pray, and ask, "God, how should I respond?"

Closing Prayer: *Lord, thank You for creating emotions. Help me to manage them wisely and not let them control me. When I feel over-whelmed, remind me to turn to You. Give me wisdom to respond with grace and patience. Teach me to reflect Your love in how I handle my emotions, and to seek peace instead of conflict. Amen.*

WEEK 17
OVERCOMING FEAR & WORRY

START DATE: _____

Bible Verse: *"Do not be anxious about anything, but in every situation, by prayer and petition, with thanksgiving, present your requests to God."* — Philippians 4:6 (NIV)

Devotional Message:

Fear and worry can show up without warning. Maybe you're afraid of failing, of not being enough, or of what the future might hold. When things feel out of your control, anxiety has a way of taking over—clouding your thoughts and making peace feel far away. But you don't have to carry that weight alone.

God never promised we wouldn't face fear, but He did promise that we can bring every anxious thought to Him. He invites us to come to Him in every situation—not just the big crises, but the small worries too. When we turn to Him with a heart of trust and thankfulness, we make space for His peace to enter in.

His peace doesn't mean all our problems disappear—it means we no longer face them alone. When you lean into God instead of your fears, He becomes your steady anchor.

Fear often whispers lies. It says you're alone, that no one understands, and that things will never get better. But God says something different. He says, "I am with you." He says, "You are never alone." In Isaiah 41:10, He promises to strengthen and help you. That's a truth you can hold onto when your mind starts to spiral.

Think about Esther. She faced a terrifying decision: stay silent and stay safe, or risk her life to speak up for her people. Fear could have paralyzed her, but instead of acting out of anxiety, she paused to fast and pray (Esther 4:15–16). She sought God's guidance and moved forward with courage. Her peace didn't come from knowing everything would work out—it came from knowing she wasn't facing it alone.

So what does it look like to trust God when you're anxious? Start with prayer. Even a short, simple cry for help can bring peace. Surround yourself with Scripture—verses that remind you of God's presence and faithfulness. When worry creeps in, pause and refocus. You don't have to solve everything at once. God will walk with you one step at a time.

Fear might not vanish instantly, but it will lose its grip when you bring it to God.

His peace isn't based on circumstances—it comes from knowing you're safe in His hands.

Reflection Questions:

1. What is something you've been worrying about lately?
2. How can you remind yourself to pray when fear creeps in?
3. What Bible verse can you memorize to help overcome worry?

Challenge for the Week: Every time you start to worry this week, stop and pray. Give your fears to God and remind yourself of His promises.

Closing Prayer: *Lord, I give my fears and worries to You. Help me to trust that You are in control, even when life feels uncertain. When I start to feel anxious, remind me to turn to You instead of letting fear take over. Fill my heart with Your peace and teach me to walk in faith. Amen.*

WEEK 18

THE BEAUTY OF PATIENCE

START DATE: _____

Bible Verse: *"But if we hope for what we do not yet have, we wait for it patiently."* — Romans 8:25 (NIV)

Devotional Message:

Waiting is hard. Whether you're waiting for a prayer to be answered, a dream to come true, or simply for a hard season to end, patience doesn't always come naturally. In a world where every-thing moves fast—texts, downloads, overnight shipping—it's easy to get frustrated when life doesn't follow your timeline.

But often, the most important growth happens during the wait.

Waiting with hope means trusting that God is working behind the scenes, even when nothing seems to be happening. It's not passive or pointless. It's active trust. And while waiting can feel like a delay, God uses it to prepare, strengthen, and refine us. Waiting is not wasted when it draws you closer to Him.

Abraham and Sarah understood what it meant to wait. God promised them a child, but years passed with no answer. They wrestled with doubt, tried to take matters into their own hands, and still the promise didn't come right away. But when the time was right—long after it seemed possible—God fulfilled what He said He would (*Genesis 21:1–2*). Their story reminds us that God's promises are never late. Delay doesn't mean denial; it means He's still working.

When you're stuck in a season of waiting, it's tempting to take control or lose hope. But forcing something before it's time often leads to disappointment. Instead of rushing ahead, learn to lean into the process. Waiting gives you space to listen, to grow, and to deepen your dependence on God.

If you're struggling to wait well, try shifting your mindset. Rather than asking, *Why is this taking so long?* ask, *What might God be teaching me right now?*

Stay committed to the small things in front of you. Do your best where you are, even if it doesn't feel like much. Trust that God's timing isn't just good—it's perfect.

Patience doesn't mean pretending the wait is easy. It means choosing peace in the unknown, hope in the silence, and trust in the One who holds your future.

He sees the whole picture, and He hasn't forgotten you. You're not stuck—you're being shaped.

Reflection Questions:

1. Is there something in your life that you've been waiting on? How can you trust God with it?
2. Why do you think patience is so difficult?
3. How can you remind yourself that God is working, even when you don't see it?

Challenge for the Week: The next time you feel impatient, pause and pray. Ask God to help you trust His timing and to grow your patience in the process.

Closing Prayer: *Lord, I know Your timing is perfect, even when I don't understand it. Help me to be patient and trust that You are working in my waiting. Teach me to rely on You instead of rushing ahead. Strengthen my faith as I wait for Your best. Amen.*

WEEK 19

YOUR INFLUENCE MATTERS

START DATE: _____

Bible Verse: *"Let your light shine before others, that they may see your good deeds and glorify your Father in heaven."* — Matthew 5:16 (NIV)

Devotional Message:

Whether you realize it or not, you're setting an example. Your actions, words, and even your attitude leave an impression on the people around you—friends, classmates, siblings, teammates. Every day, your choices tell a story about what you value and who you follow.

Influence isn't about popularity or having a platform. It's about showing up with kindness, living with integrity, and choosing what's right even when it's hard.

People notice when you encourage someone who's having a rough day, refuse to gossip, or speak up for someone being treated unfairly. These simple moments can quietly point others toward God.

Think about someone who's made a lasting impact on you. Maybe it was a coach who believed in you, a friend who stuck by you, or someone who helped you feel seen and valued. Their influence didn't come from being perfect—it came from showing love, honesty, and faithfulness in ordinary moments. That's the same kind of influence you're called to carry.

Scripture also warns that influence can go both ways. The people you surround yourself with shape how you think, act, and grow. If you're constantly around negativity or compromise, it can slowly wear you down. That doesn't mean cutting people off, but it does mean being wise about who you allow to shape your heart.

God wants you to be the kind of friend who builds others up—and to choose friends who do the same for you.

You don't need to pretend to have it all together. What matters most is consistency. Living with purpose. Being real. Staying rooted in your faith when it's tempting to blend in. When others see you choosing forgiveness over anger, joy over complaining, or truth over fitting in, you're shining your light.

Your influence won't always be loud or obvious—but it's powerful. In a world full of comparison and pressure, living for God stands out. And when people notice that difference, they won't just admire you—they may begin to wonder about the God who guides you.

Reflection Questions:

1. Who has been a positive influence in your life? How did they impact you?
2. How can you be more intentional about influencing others in a way that honors God?
3. Are there any negative influences in your life that you need to set boundaries with?

Challenge for the Week: Be intentional about using your influence for good. Find one way each day to encourage, support, or uplift someone around you.

Closing Prayer: *Lord, help me to be a light for others. Let my words and actions reflect Your love and truth. Give me wisdom to choose good influences and to be a positive influence in the lives of those around me. Use me to lead others closer to You. Amen.*

WEEK 20

TAKING RESPONSIBILITY

START DATE: _____

Bible Verse: *"Each of you should carry your own load."* — Galatians 6:5 (NIV)

Devotional Message:

When something goes wrong, it's easy to point fingers. Maybe someone let you down in a group project, a friend misunderstood your words, or you forgot a responsibility and tried to shift the blame. That gut reaction—*It's not my fault*—is something we've all felt. But growing in faith means learning to say something harder and more honest: *I was wrong. I should have handled that differently.*

Taking responsibility isn't about beating yourself up. It's about being mature enough to recognize your part in a situation and willing to make it right. It shows strength, not weakness. Blaming others may offer short-term relief, but it doesn't lead to real growth. Ownership does. And the more you practice it, the easier it becomes to choose humility over pride.

King David's story shows what this looks like. After he made a series of terrible choices involving Bathsheba and her husband, he was confronted by the prophet Nathan (*2 Samuel 12*). David didn't hide behind his power or make excuses—he confessed his sin openly. His willingness to admit fault, even after a massive failure, opened the door for repentance, healing, and restoration. And despite everything, God still called David a man after His own heart (*Acts 13:22*). Why? Because David was humble enough to take responsibility.

In everyday life, this might mean apologizing when you've hurt someone, even if it was unintentional. It might mean admitting you didn't give your best effort, or stepping up when you've fallen short. It also means following through on what you say you'll do. When you live with integrity—doing your part, owning your choices—you build trust with others and with God. And over time, people come to see you as dependable, sincere, and strong in character.

But this isn't just about actions—it's also about your faith. No one else can follow Jesus for you. Your parents, friends, or youth leaders can support and encourage you, but at the end of the day, your relationship with God is your own. Choosing to grow spiritually, to pray, to learn, to worship—these are your steps to take.

God doesn't expect perfection, but He does invite honesty. And when you're willing to own your part, He meets you with grace and helps you move forward stronger.

Reflection Questions:

1. Why is it so tempting to blame others when something goes wrong?
2. What's one area of your life where you need to take more responsibility?
3. How can taking ownership of your actions help you grow spiritually?

Challenge for the Week: Choose one area where you've been making excuses or shifting blame. Own it, pray about it, and take one step toward making it right.

Closing Prayer: *Lord, give me the courage to take responsibility for my actions. Help me to be honest with others and with You. Teach me to grow from my mistakes instead of hiding them. Thank You for offering grace and a fresh start when I mess up. Amen.*

WEEK 21

HANDLING CRITICISM WITH GRACE

START DATE: _____

Bible Verse: *"A gentle answer turns away wrath, but a harsh word stirs up anger."* — Proverbs 15:1 (NIV)

Devotional Message:

No one enjoys being corrected. Whether the feedback comes from a teacher, parent, coach, or friend, it can sting—especially when you've tried your best or didn't realize you'd done something wrong. The natural reaction is to get defensive, explain yourself, or even snap back. But God invites you to respond differently—with gentleness, humility, and grace.

How you respond to criticism matters. It's not just about what was said to you, but about the posture of your heart in that moment. A quick, harsh comeback might feel satisfying in the moment, but it rarely brings peace. A gentle answer has the power to calm the situation and leave space for understanding and growth. Responding with grace can be the very thing that opens the door to deeper connection and healing.

Jesus is the ultimate example of this. Throughout His ministry, He was constantly questioned, challenged, and criticized—especially by the Pharisees (*Matthew 12:14, Mark 2:16–28, Luke 11:53–54*). But He never let anger take over. His responses were thoughtful, calm, and full of truth. He knew who He was, and that allowed Him to respond from a place of strength, not insecurity.

It's also important to understand that not all criticism is the same. Some of it is helpful—even if it's uncomfortable to hear. A trusted friend might gently point out something that could help you grow. A mentor might give feedback that sharpens your character. These moments are opportunities for God to shape you.

Then there's criticism that's simply mean-spirited or unfair. Maybe someone is tearing you down to make themselves feel better or spreading negativity without knowing the full story. In those moments, remember that your worth doesn't come from what others say about you—it comes from what God says about you.

The key is knowing when to receive correction and when to let go of criticism that isn't rooted in love. Take a breath before you respond. Ask God for discernment. If there's truth in what's being said, take it to heart and grow from it. If it's meant to harm, don't let it settle in your spirit.

God can use both encouragement and correction to build you into the person He's called you to be. Stay teachable, stay kind, and trust that He's shaping your heart every step of the way.

Reflection Questions:

1. How do you usually react when someone corrects you?
2. How can you tell the difference between helpful and hurtful criticism?
3. What is one way you can respond with grace the next time you receive criticism?

Challenge for the Week: The next time you receive criticism, pause before responding. If it's helpful, thank the person and learn from it. If it's hurtful, pray about it and choose to let it go.

Closing Prayer: *Lord, help me to handle criticism with grace. Give me humility to learn from correction and strength to ignore negativity. Remind me that my worth is in You, not in the opinions of others. Let my words and reactions reflect Your wisdom and love. Amen.*

WEEK 22

BREAKING FREE FROM NEGATIVE PATTERNS

START DATE: _____

Bible Verse: *"No temptation has overtaken you except what is common to mankind. And God is faithful; he will not let you be tempted beyond what you can bear. But when you are tempted, he will also provide a way out so that you can endure it."* — 1 Corinthians 10:13 (NIV)

Devotional Message:

Bad habits can feel like chains—quietly holding you back, even when you want to move forward. Maybe it's procrastination, negativity, gossip, comparison, or something more private. You tell yourself, *This is the last time,* but before you know it, you're stuck in the same cycle again. That can be frustrating and discouraging. But here's the hope: you are not alone in your struggle, and you are not powerless to change.

God never promised we wouldn't face temptation, but He did promise we'd never face it without a way out. You're not the only one battling certain patterns—what you're facing is part of the human experience. And the same God who sees your heart also gives you strength to resist and the wisdom to walk away. He is not disappointed in your struggle—He is present in it, ready to help you overcome.

Even Paul, the apostle who wrote much of the New Testament, admitted that he struggled with doing the right thing. In *Romans 7:15*, he said, *"I do not understand what I do. For what I want to do I do not do, but what I hate I do."* That level of honesty shows that even those with great faith face real inner battles.

Breaking free doesn't happen all at once. It starts with recognizing the habit and naming it. Not in shame, but in truth. God already knows—and He still chooses to walk with you. Change also requires dependence. Willpower alone will get you only so far. But when you turn to God in prayer and invite Him into your weakness, you open the door to real transformation.

Replacing old patterns with new ones can make a big difference. Instead of letting negativity take over, choose one kind thing to say each day. Instead of spiraling into comparison, take a moment to thank God for something uniquely yours.

And don't walk this path alone. Find someone you trust—a parent, mentor, or friend—who will check in with you and cheer you on. Accountability doesn't mean judgment; it means support and encouragement when the journey gets hard.

God never sees you as a lost cause. He sees your effort, your desire to grow, and your willingness to keep trying. Every day is another opportunity to take one step forward—and every step counts.

Reflection Questions:

1. What bad habit do you struggle with the most?
2. How can you rely on God to help you overcome it?
3. What positive habit can you replace it with?

Challenge for the Week: Identify one habit you need to break. Pray about it daily and take one small step toward change.

Closing Prayer: *Lord, I know there are habits in my life that I need to let go of. Give me the strength to break free and the wisdom to replace them with habits that honor You. Thank You for always providing a way out. Help me to walk in Your strength, not my own. Amen.*

PART THREE
FRIENDSHIPS, RELATIONSHIPS & SERVING OTHERS

WEEK 23

CHOOSING FRIENDS WISELY

START DATE: _____

Bible Verse: *"Walk with the wise and become wise, for a companion of fools suffers harm."* — Proverbs 13:20 (NIV)

Devotional Message:

Friends have a huge impact on your life. They can encourage you, help you grow in your faith, and be there when life gets hard. But they can also distract you from God, pull you into gossip or drama, or push you toward choices you know aren't right. That's why the people you choose to keep close matter so much.

The people around you shape who you're becoming. If your closest friends are kind, wise, and seeking God, that influence will rub off on you. But if they're always negative, careless, or dragging you into situations that make you feel guilty afterward, that influence can pull you further from the person you want to be. Sometimes, your environment shapes you more than you realize.

Even Jesus was intentional with His friendships. He showed love to everyone—He talked to the outcasts, dined with sinners, and welcomed the broken. But His closest friends, like Peter, James, and John, were people who shared His purpose. They weren't perfect, but they were walking in the same direction. Jesus didn't isolate

Himself, but He also didn't let unhealthy relationships shape His mission.

So what kind of friends do you have? Do they push you closer to God or distract you from Him? Do they lift you up or bring you down? And what kind of friend are you in return? Friendship is a two-way street. If you want to have godly friendships, you need to be a godly friend—honest, kind, loyal, and loving, even when it's hard.

This doesn't mean you should stop caring about people who are struggling or who believe differently than you. Jesus calls you to love everyone. But loving people doesn't mean giving everyone access to your inner circle. It's okay—and wise—to set boundaries with people who consistently pull you into negativity, pressure you to compromise, or steer you away from God's best.

When you walk with the wise, you grow in wisdom. When you surround yourself with friends who reflect God's love, it becomes easier to live it out yourself.

Friendships are powerful—so choose them prayerfully.

Reflection Questions:

1. How have your closest friends influenced you—positively or negatively?
2. Are there any friendships in your life that may be pulling you away from God?
3. How can you be a better friend to those around you?

Challenge for the Week: Evaluate your friendships. If someone is leading you away from God, pray for wisdom on how to handle that relationship. Look for ways to be a positive influence in your friend group.

Closing Prayer: *Lord, thank You for the friendships in my life. Help me to choose friends who encourage me in my faith and challenge me to be better. Give me wisdom to set boundaries where needed, and help me to be a friend who reflects Your love. Amen.*

WEEK 24

RESPECTING YOURSELF & OTHERS

START DATE: _____

Bible Verse: *"Be devoted to one another in love. Honor one another above yourselves."* — Romans 12:10 (NIV)

Devotional Message:

Relationships shape a lot of who you are. Whether it's with friends, family, teammates, or classmates, the way you treat others—and the way they treat you—has a lasting impact.

That's why God cares so deeply about how you love and respect the people around you.

Respect isn't just about using good manners or being polite when you have to. It's about truly seeing the value in others—recognizing their worth as people created by God. That kind of love shows up in how you listen, how you speak, how you handle conflict, and even how you set boundaries.

Jesus modeled respect in powerful ways. He honored people who were often ignored or looked down on. He saw the worth of each person—rich or poor, strong or struggling—and treated them with dignity and grace. Even when others disrespected Him, He responded with wisdom and love.

So what does a healthy, respectful relationship actually look like? It's mutual. Real friendships don't ask you to change who you are to be accepted—they celebrate who God made you to be. They encourage you to grow, speak life into you, and challenge you to become better. If someone constantly puts you down, pressures you to compromise, or drains your energy without giving anything in return, that's a sign something's off.

Respect also means knowing when to step back. You can be kind and loving while still setting boundaries with people who are consistently negative or hurtful. Jesus showed love to everyone, but He also protected His purpose by not letting others steer Him off course.

And respect doesn't stop with your closest relationships. It also applies to how you treat your parents, teachers, and even people you might not agree with. Choosing to honor others—even when it's inconvenient or uncomfortable—reflects God's love in a powerful way.

You don't have to get every relationship perfect. But with God's help, you can aim to build connections that are healthy, loving, and grounded in grace.

Reflection Questions:

1. Are your friendships and relationships built on mutual respect?
2. How can you better show respect to those around you?
3. Do you need to set boundaries with anyone who is negatively influencing you?

Challenge for the Week: Be intentional about showing respect this week. Whether it's being patient with family, listening more, or choosing kindness in a disagreement, let your actions reflect God's love.

Closing Prayer: *Lord, help me to build healthy relationships that honor You. Teach me to respect others, even when it's difficult, and give me wisdom to set boundaries when needed. Let my words and actions reflect Your love and grace. Amen.*

WEEK 25

DEALING WITH PEER PRESSURE

START DATE: _____

Bible Verse: *"Do not follow the crowd in doing wrong."* — Exodus 23:2a (NIV)

Devotional Message:

Have you ever felt pressured to go along with something you knew wasn't right—just to fit in or avoid being the odd one out? Maybe it was gossiping, lying, sneaking something past your parents, or staying silent when you should have spoken up. That's peer pressure, and it can show up in both obvious and subtle ways.

It doesn't always come as someone telling you what to do. Sometimes it's a smirk, a comment like "It's not a big deal," or the fear of being excluded if you don't join in. But deep inside, you often know when something doesn't feel right. That's the Holy Spirit prompting you to hold on to your values.

Just because "everyone else is doing it" doesn't mean it's right. It takes strength to resist the crowd, but God calls you to walk in integrity, even when it's hard. Being different can feel lonely, but it's also powerful—and it honors God. Even a quiet decision to say no can speak volumes about your character and your faith.

Daniel is a great example of someone who stood firm under pressure. When he was taken to Babylon, he was offered food and customs that went against God's laws. Instead of blending in, he chose to stay faithful—even when it set him apart (Daniel 1:8). He didn't make a scene, but he respectfully stood his ground. God honored that bold decision and used Daniel's faith to influence an entire kingdom.

Resisting peer pressure starts before you're in the moment. The more grounded you are in God's Word, the easier it is to recognize when something is off. And remember: you don't need to explain yourself to everyone. A calm "No thanks" is often all it takes. True friends will respect your values—even if they don't share them. And if they don't, it's worth asking whether those friendships are helping you grow or holding you back.

Surround yourself with people who support your convictions. When you face tough situations, pray right in the moment—God will give you the courage to walk away, speak up, or simply stand firm. Every time you choose what's right, you grow stronger in your faith. Your boldness could be the encouragement someone else needs.

Reflection Questions:

1. When have you felt pressured to do something you knew was wrong?
2. What helped (or would have helped) you say no in that moment?
3. How can you prepare now to stand strong the next time peer pressure shows up?

Challenge for the Week: When you feel pressure to go along with something wrong, pause and pray. Ask God for strength to do what's right—even if you're the only one.

Closing Prayer: *God, give me courage to stand for what's right, even when others don't. Help me to recognize peer pressure and respond with wisdom and strength. Let my choices honor You and influence others in a positive way. Amen.*

WEEK 26
FINDING MENTORS & ROLE MODELS

START DATE: _____

Bible Verse: *"Listen to advice and accept discipline, and at the end you will be counted among the wise."* — Proverbs 19:20 (NIV)

Devotional Message:

You don't have to figure out life on your own. God places people in your life—parents, teachers, coaches, youth leaders—not to control you, but to guide and support you. Mentors are people who've walked ahead of you in life and faith, and they can offer wisdom, encouragement, and truth right when you need it most.

It takes humility to listen, but being open to advice leads to growth. Mentors help you see things you might miss and gently correct you when you're heading down the wrong path. The wisest people aren't those who have all the answers—they're the ones willing to keep learning and growing with guidance.

Throughout the Bible, God used mentor relationships to shape the next generation of leaders. Moses prepared Joshua to lead Israel after him (Deuteronomy 31:7–8). Naomi guided Ruth through grief and into hope (Ruth 1–4). Paul encouraged Timothy in his calling to preach and lead, even when Timothy felt young and uncertain (1 Timothy 4:12, 2 Timothy 1:5–7). And Jesus spent years walking alongside His disciples—teaching, correcting, and equipping them to live out God's truth.

These relationships weren't perfect, but they were rooted in love, honesty, and purpose. God designed us to grow through connection, not isolation.

Maybe you don't have a mentor right now, and that's okay. Start by praying for one. God may already have placed someone in your life who's ready to support you—a teacher who notices when you're struggling, a youth leader who checks in after church, or a family member who lives out their faith in quiet, steady ways.

At the same time, you might already be a mentor to someone and not even realize it. Every time you encourage a younger sibling, help a friend stay on the right path, or live out your faith with kindness, you're setting an example someone else can follow.

If you want to grow through mentorship, be willing to listen—even when the advice is hard to hear. Be honest about your struggles, and stay open to learning from others. The people who challenge you with truth often care the most.

Wisdom grows in community. And with the right people by your side, you'll gain not only insight—but strength, courage, and purpose for the road ahead.

Reflection Questions:

1. Is there someone in your life who's been a mentor to you? What have you learned from them?
2. Why is it hard sometimes to accept advice or correction?
3. How can you be a positive example for someone else?

Challenge for the Week: Reach out to someone you admire in faith. Ask for advice, share a struggle, or simply thank them for being an example in your life.

Closing Prayer: *Lord, thank You for the people who guide and support me. Help me to be humble and willing to learn. Bring mentors into my life who will help me grow, and teach me how to be a light for others as well. Amen.*

WEEK 27
RESOLVING CONFLICT WITH LOVE

START DATE: _____

Bible Verse: *"If it is possible, as far as it depends on you, live at peace with everyone."* — Romans 12:18 (NIV)

Devotional Message:

Conflict is part of life. Whether it's a fight with a friend, a misunderstanding with your parents, or drama at school, we all run into situations where people disagree. But God doesn't call us to win arguments—He calls us to respond with love.

You can't control what others do, but you can choose your response. Even when you're hurt or frustrated, God asks you to lead with kindness and grace. Living at peace doesn't mean pretending everything's fine or avoiding tough conversations. It means choosing a gentle, honest, and loving approach, even when it's hard. That kind of response takes strength and spiritual maturity—and it sets you apart.

Jesus faced constant conflict—people questioned Him, misunderstood Him, and even plotted against Him. Yet He stayed calm, stood firm in truth, and responded with compassion. He didn't avoid hard conversations, but He always spoke with love and purpose. His peace wasn't weakness—it was strength rooted in God.

Sometimes we'd rather avoid someone or lash out to defend ourselves. But when we resolve conflict the right way—with love, humility, and forgiveness—it can actually bring people closer.

It shows strength, not weakness, to be a peacemaker.

It also takes courage to take the first step. Maybe the other person isn't ready to talk, or maybe they don't see the problem the same way you do. Still, your effort matters to God. He sees when you choose grace instead of bitterness, and He honors your heart for peace. Even small acts of humility can soften hearts and change the atmosphere.

So how can you resolve conflict with love? Pause before reacting and pray. Be honest, but kind. Listen before you judge. Own your part, and be willing to forgive. These choices might not fix everything right away, but they open the door to healing. And every time you choose love, you're building stronger relationships and becoming more like Jesus.

Not every situation will turn out perfectly. But when you choose peace over pride, and love over being right, you reflect the heart of Christ—and that can make a real difference.

Reflection Questions:

1. How do you usually respond when you're in conflict with someone?
2. Is there a relationship in your life that needs healing right now?
3. What step can you take to approach conflict with more love and humility?

Challenge for the Week: Think of someone you've had tension with lately. Pray about it, then take one step toward peace—whether it's apologizing, listening, or simply choosing not to hold a grudge.

Closing Prayer: *Lord, help me to handle conflict with love. Give me the humility to listen, the wisdom to speak with kindness, and the courage to forgive. Teach me to be a peacemaker who reflects Your grace. Amen.*

WEEK 28

A HEART LIKE HIS

START DATE: _____

Bible Verse: "Do nothing out of selfish ambition or vain conceit. Rather, in humility value others above yourselves." — Philippians 2:3 (NIV)

Devotional Message:

When you picture someone serving others, you might imagine big, impressive acts—building homes, leading fundraisers, or going on mission trips. Those things matter. But the kind of service Jesus modeled didn't always look dramatic. Most often, it looked like quiet humility: noticing people, putting others first, and doing small things with great love.

Jesus didn't seek attention. He didn't help people to boost His reputation or wait for perfect conditions. He served constantly, with a heart that was open, gentle, and focused on others. One of His most powerful examples wasn't a miracle—it was when He washed His disciples' feet, taking the position of a servant (John 13:14–15). In that moment, He showed that real greatness comes through humility.

You don't need a title, platform, or applause to live like Jesus. You serve when you help your sibling without being asked. When you choose to sit with the new student instead of your usual group.

When you put your phone down and really listen. When you forgive quickly and show kindness without expecting anything back. That's what it means to live with a servant's heart.

The world often tells you to put yourself first—but God's Word teaches something better. Service isn't weakness—it's strength rooted in love. It takes courage to let go of pride, to value others above yourself, and to do what's right even when no one notices. Serving others means being willing to be inconvenienced, even when it costs you time or comfort.

Ask God to give you His heart—a heart that's quick to notice, slow to judge, and ready to love. When you approach your everyday life with a posture of humility, you'll start to see service opportunities all around you. And as you serve, your own heart will grow softer, stronger, and more like His.

You don't have to change the world to reflect Jesus. Just live with love, live with humility—and trust that God is using your small acts of service to do something bigger than you can imagine.

Reflection Questions:

1. What's one small way you can serve someone in your daily routine this week?
2. Do you struggle more with humility or with feeling like your service doesn't matter? Why?
3. Who in your life has shown you what it looks like to serve with love?

Challenge for the Week: Each day this week, find one quiet way to serve someone around you—without expecting recognition. Keep a simple journal of how it made you feel and where you saw God in the process.

Closing Prayer: *Jesus, thank You for showing me that real greatness starts with humility. Give me a heart like Yours—one that sees people, serves with love, and doesn't need a spotlight. Help me to value others above myself and to find joy in loving well, even in the smallest ways. Amen.*

WEEK 29

HOW TO APOLOGIZE & MAKE THINGS RIGHT

START DATE: _____

Bible Verse: *"Therefore confess your sins to each other and pray for each other so that you may be healed."* — James 5:16a (NIV)

Devotional Message:

Everyone messes up. Whether you said something hurtful, broke a promise, or let someone down, we all have moments where our words or actions cause pain. What matters most isn't being perfect —it's what you do after the mistake. And one of the most powerful things you can do is offer a genuine apology.

That word *"confess"* in James 5:16 is key. It means being honest about what you did wrong—not blaming, excusing, or hiding it. When you take responsibility, healing can begin—for you and the person you hurt.

A real apology isn't just saying "sorry" to move on. It's about understanding how your actions affected someone else and doing your part to make it right. That kind of humility takes courage—but it's also what builds stronger, healthier relationships. People may forget what you said, but they'll remember how you handled it when you were wrong. Apologizing well shows others that you value them more than your pride or reputation.

Think about Zacchaeus in *Luke 19*. After encountering Jesus, he realized how much harm he had caused. He didn't just say sorry—he made things right by repaying what he had taken and more. His actions showed that his heart had truly changed. A changed heart always leads to changed behavior.

So what does a real apology look like?

• *Be specific.* Don't just say, "I'm sorry if I hurt you." Say, "I'm sorry for what I said. It was wrong, and I understand it hurt you."

• *Don't shift blame.* Own your part without excuses.

• *Listen.* Let the other person share how they feel, and be willing to hear them.

• *Make it right.* If there's a way to rebuild trust, take it seriously.

• *Ask God to help.* He can give you the humility and wisdom you need.

Apologizing may feel uncomfortable, but it brings peace and healing. It takes strength to say, *"I was wrong,"* and even more strength to ask, *"How can I make it right?"* But when you do, you reflect God's love at work in your life—and you become someone others can trust.

A sincere apology can be the first step in repairing what was broken and opening the door to something even better than before.

Reflection Questions:

1. Is there someone you need to apologize to?
2. Why is it sometimes hard to admit when we're wrong?
3. How does owning your actions show spiritual maturity?

Challenge for the Week: If you've hurt someone, take the first step toward healing. Apologize honestly, without excuses, and ask God to guide your next steps.

Closing Prayer: *Lord, help me to be honest about my mistakes. Give me the humility to apologize and the wisdom to make things right. Teach me to care more about healing relationships than protecting my pride. Amen.*

WEEK 30

AVOIDING GOSSIP & DRAMA

START DATE: _____

Bible Verse: *"Without wood a fire goes out; without a gossip a quarrel dies down."* — Proverbs 26:20 (NIV)

Devotional Message:

Gossip might seem harmless at first. It can feel like you're just sharing a funny story or venting about something that happened. But gossip spreads quickly, cuts deeply, and fuels unnecessary drama. And once it's said, you can't take it back.

Just like fire needs wood to keep burning, gossip fuels conflict. But when you choose not to speak negatively—or even to listen—you pull the fuel away. That small decision can help bring peace and stop the cycle before it causes more damage.

Jesus never gossiped. Even when people failed, betrayed, or misunderstood Him, He didn't use their mistakes as material for casual conversation. He treated every person with dignity and handled truth with love. That's the example we're meant to follow. Gossip may feel small, but it reflects the condition of our hearts. Are we using our words to build others up—or to tear them down?

It's not just about what we say—it's also about what we allow. Listening to gossip without speaking up makes us part of the problem. And people who gossip to you are often willing to gossip about you.

Choosing to walk away or steer the conversation in a better direction takes courage, but it sets you apart as someone who values peace and integrity.

Avoiding gossip doesn't mean pretending everything is fine or ignoring real issues. There are times you may need to talk through a situation with a trusted adult or mentor to find clarity or healing. The difference is your motive. Are you seeking wisdom—or spreading drama?

And when you've been the one gossiped about, you know how painful it feels to be misunderstood or misrepresented. That reminder should make us all more careful with how we speak about others.

The words you choose shape how others see you. When you speak life instead of fueling conflict, you become a safe place for others. You reflect Jesus not just in what you believe, but in how you talk. And that's one of the most powerful ways to show His love in your everyday life.

Reflection Questions:

1. Have you ever been hurt by gossip? How did it feel?
2. What can you do when you're tempted to join in on gossip?
3. How can you be a peacemaker in your friend group this week?

Challenge for the Week: The next time someone starts gossiping, choose not to join in. Steer the conversation in a better direction or walk away. Be the one who ends the drama, not the one who fuels it.

Closing Prayer: *Lord, help me to guard my words and choose kindness over gossip. Give me courage to speak life, not harm, and to be someone others can trust. Teach me to bring peace into my conversations and reflect Your love in how I speak. Amen.*

WEEK 31

DATING WITH WISDOM AND WORTH

BIBLE VERSE: *"Above all else, guard your heart, for everything you do flows from it."* — Proverbs 4:23 (NIV)

Devotional Message:

Dating can be exciting, confusing, and emotional—all at once. You might wonder what's "normal," what's healthy, and how to hold onto your faith when feelings are strong. Culture says love is all about butterflies, drama, or how far you're willing to go. But God's version of love looks different—and better.

Real love starts with wisdom. *Proverbs 4:23* tells us to guard our hearts, not because love is bad, but because it's powerful. Your heart matters to God, and how you handle it in dating relationships matters too. When you date with wisdom, you protect what's sacred, and you invite God into the process.

Godly love isn't reckless or controlling—it's patient, kind, honest, and respectful (*1 Corinthians 13:4–7*). It doesn't rush or pressure. It doesn't use flattery to manipulate. It values who you are, not just how you look or what you can offer. *Song of Songs 2:7* even says not to "awaken love before it's time," because love grows best when it's rooted in trust and timing, not pressure or impulse. That kind of love builds trust, not anxiety.

Dating with wisdom also means paying attention to red flags. Does this person draw you closer to God—or pull you away? Do they respect your values and boundaries—or push past them? Are you free to be honest—or do you feel like you have to change who you are just to keep their interest? These questions don't make you picky —they make you wise.

You don't have to date just because everyone else is. And your worth isn't measured by whether you've had a boyfriend, been asked out, or gotten attention online. You are complete in Christ— not because of who likes you, but because of who loves you first (*Romans 5:8*).

If you do feel ready to date, invite God into it from the very beginning. Ask Him to guide your heart, your decisions, and your pace. Talk to someone you trust—like a mentor, parent, or youth leader— who can walk with you through it. You don't have to figure it out alone.

Dating doesn't have to mean drama, confusion, or compromise. With God's wisdom, it can be something that builds you up—not tears you down.

Reflection Questions:

1. What kind of qualities do you think godly love should have?
2. Are there any red flags you've ignored—or green flags you want to look for?
3. How can you guard your heart and honor God whether you're dating or not?

Challenge for the Week: Make a list of five qualities you want in a future dating relationship—things that honor God, not just what looks good on the outside. Pray over the list and ask God to shape your view of love.

Closing Prayer: *God, thank You for loving me perfectly. Help me to walk in wisdom when it comes to dating. Teach me to guard my heart, honor You in my choices, and trust that Your plan for love is better than anything the world offers. Amen.*

WEEK 32

THE STRENGTH TO SAY NO

START DATE: _____

Bible Verse: *"It is God's will that you should be sanctified: that you should avoid sexual immorality; that each of you should learn to control your own body in a way that is holy and honorable."* — 1 Thessalonians 4:3–4 (NIV)

Devotional Message:

Romantic attention can feel exciting. Maybe someone compliments you, texts you often, or makes you feel seen in a way no one else has. But sometimes, that attention comes with pressure—pressure to go further than you're ready for physically or emotionally. Saying "no" in those moments isn't easy, but it's one of the strongest things you can do.

God created romantic attraction, and it's not wrong to want to be loved or desired. But His design for love includes boundaries that protect your heart, body, and future. The world says, "If it feels good, do it." God says, "You are worth more than a moment." You are not defined by someone else's desires, but by God's purpose for your life. Your value doesn't increase or decrease based on someone's attention.

1 Thessalonians 4 reminds us that God wants us to live in a way that is holy and honorable—to treat our bodies with care and expect that

73

same respect from others. That includes saying no when someone tries to cross a line, even if they say they care about you. Real love doesn't pressure or guilt—it honors.

You might worry that saying no will make someone leave. And sometimes they will. But that doesn't mean you're wrong. It means you're making space for love that honors God—and you. Choosing to wait doesn't mean you're missing out—it means you're protecting what matters most.

If you've ever said yes when you wish you hadn't, know this: God's grace is real, and His love for you hasn't changed. You can start fresh today. He cares more about your heart than your history.

So how do you stand strong when pressure is real? Know what you believe and why it matters. Set clear boundaries—and don't be afraid to walk away from someone who won't respect them. Surround yourself with people who remind you of your worth.

Saying no doesn't make you weak or stuck-up. It makes you wise, courageous, and free. And it shows that your heart belongs first to the One who made it.

Reflection Questions:

1. Have you ever felt pressured to cross a boundary— physically or emotionally—in a relationship?
2. What are some personal boundaries you want to set or protect?
3. How can you remind yourself of your worth when you feel uncertain?

Challenge for the Week: Write a list of personal boundaries you'd like to keep in dating relationships—physical, emotional, or spiritual. Pray over them, and ask God to help you honor those boundaries and give you courage to say no when needed.

Closing Prayer: *God, thank You for creating me with value and purpose. Help me to say no to anything that dishonors You or pressures me to compromise. Give me wisdom, strength, and peace in moments of uncertainty, and remind me that I am already fully loved by You. Amen.*

WEEK 33

HONORING PARENTS & AUTHORITY

START DATE: _____

Bible Verse: *"Honor your father and your mother, so that you may live long in the land the Lord your God is giving you."* — Exodus 20:12 (NIV)

Devotional Message:

Let's be honest—honoring parents and authority figures isn't always easy. Maybe your parents set rules you don't agree with. Maybe a teacher or coach seems unfair or quick to judge. But even when it's hard, God calls us to honor those He's placed in our lives.

To honor means to show respect and value. It's more than just obedience—it's about attitude. You can follow the rules but still roll your eyes, talk back, or hold resentment. Honoring comes from the heart and flows from a desire to please God, not just people. It shows trust in His wisdom, even when your emotions don't line up. And over time, that kind of respect can strengthen relationships and build deeper trust.

Jesus gave us the perfect example. Even though He was the Son of God, He honored His earthly parents. In Luke 2, after being found in the temple, He went home with Mary and Joseph and obeyed them (*Luke 2:51*). And when He stood before leaders who mocked

Him, He didn't fight back—He responded with dignity and self-control.

Sometimes honoring authority means giving up your "right" to win an argument. It means learning to speak respectfully even when you're frustrated, choosing patience over sarcasm, and remembering that respect isn't earned—it's given out of love and obedience to God.

You may not always agree, but you can still choose to respond with grace.

So how do you live this out in your own life? Start by speaking respectfully, even when you're annoyed. Listen before you react. Follow through on what you're asked to do. And pray for your parents, teachers, or anyone in leadership—especially when it's hard. They're human, just like you, and they need God's help too.

Honoring authority doesn't mean accepting harmful behavior. If someone in power is acting in a way that's abusive, unsafe, or wrong, it's okay—and necessary—to speak up and get help. God cares deeply about justice and safety. But in most everyday situations, choosing honor is a way to reflect your faith and grow in maturity.

When you honor others, you're really honoring God. And that changes not just your attitude—but your whole life.

Reflection Questions:

1. What does "honoring" someone mean to you?
2. Is there a situation where you've struggled to show honor?
3. How does your attitude toward authority reflect your faith?

Challenge for the Week: Choose one authority figure in your life—like a parent or teacher—and look for a way to show honor through your words or actions this week.

Closing Prayer: *God, help me to honor the people You've placed in authority over me. Even when I don't agree, give me a heart that listens, respects, and responds with love. Teach me to lead with humility by learning how to follow well. Amen.*

WEEK 34
NAVIGATING FAMILY RELATIONSHIPS

START DATE: _____

Bible Verse: *"Bear with each other and forgive one another if any of you has a grievance against someone. Forgive as the Lord forgave you."* — Colossians 3:13 (NIV)

Devotional Message:

Family relationships can be some of the most meaningful—and the most challenging. The people we love the most are often the ones we clash with the most. Whether it's daily tension, unspoken frustration, or a misunderstanding that spiraled into something bigger, navigating family life takes grace, patience, and a whole lot of forgiveness.

Colossians 3:13 reminds us to bear with one another and to forgive, just as God forgave us. Forgiveness doesn't mean ignoring hurt or pretending things didn't happen—it means choosing to let go of bitterness and inviting God's healing into the situation. In a home, where emotions run deep and imperfections show easily, grace is essential. And while you can't change others, you can choose how you respond—with humility, love, and courage. The atmosphere in your home can begin to shift through one changed heart at a time.

Jesus knew what it was like to live in a human family. His siblings didn't always believe in Him (*John 7:5*), and He likely faced the same ups and downs of family dynamics that we do. Yet He loved faithfully, honored His parents, and showed care and compassion—even from the cross. His life gives us a model of how to love and forgive, especially when it's hard. And if Jesus made room for grace in His own family, we can too—with His help.

Living out your faith at home might look like pausing before snapping back in frustration. It might mean choosing to listen instead of assuming, or apologizing first—even if you weren't completely in the wrong. Sometimes bringing peace into your home starts with prayer. Ask God to help you see your family through His eyes and respond with His heart.

If you're facing something serious at home—like constant conflict or emotional pain—talk to someone you trust. God doesn't expect you to carry that alone, and there is strength in asking for help.

Even in a messy or imperfect family, God can use you as a source of love and light. Your quiet efforts, kind words, and willingness to forgive may be the very thing He uses to bring healing to those around you. You may not see the results right away, but small acts of love planted in faith can grow into something lasting.

Reflection Questions:

1. Who in your family do you find it hardest to show grace to —and why?
2. What's one recent moment when you could have responded differently?
3. How can God's forgiveness toward you help you offer it to someone else?

Challenge for the Week: Take one step toward healing in a family relationship—whether that's offering forgiveness, asking for it, or simply starting a kind conversation.

Closing Prayer: *God, thank You for loving me unconditionally. Help me to bring that same love into my family. Give me grace when I'm frustrated, courage when things feel hard, and a heart that's willing to forgive. Let my life reflect Your peace at home. Amen.*

WEEK 35

ENCOURAGING & LIFTING OTHERS UP

START DATE: _____

Bible Verse: *"Therefore encourage one another and build each other up, just as in fact you are doing."* — 1 Thessalonians 5:11 (NIV)

Devotional Message:

A kind word at the right moment can mean everything. Maybe someone reminded you you're not alone, or told you they believed in you when you didn't believe in yourself. Encouragement doesn't take much—but it can change everything.

We live in a world that tears people down—through criticism, comparison, and negativity. But God calls us to do the opposite. As believers, we're meant to be encouragers—people who lift others up, not pull them down. Encouraging others isn't about giving fake compliments or pretending everything's perfect. It's about noticing others, seeing the good, and choosing to speak life when you could stay silent. It means being a light in someone's dark day, even when your own isn't easy.

Jesus constantly encouraged those around Him. He lifted up the outcasts, praised people's faith, and offered hope to the hurting. Whether it was the woman at the well, the tax collector in the tree, or His tired disciples, Jesus noticed people—and reminded them they mattered. He saw past what others judged and spoke to people's potential. That kind of encouragement wasn't shallow—it was rooted in truth, love, and grace. And because Jesus lives in you, you carry that same power to speak life wherever you go.

Encouragement can be simple. It might look like texting a friend who's going through something hard, writing a note to a teacher, or choosing to say, "I'm proud of you" instead of staying quiet. Even just being present—really listening to someone or praying with them—can remind them they're not alone. And when you share Scripture, even one verse, it can bring peace and perspective to someone who's struggling.

You never know what silent battles someone is fighting, but your words might be exactly what they need to keep going. Choosing to be an encourager is one of the most powerful and Christlike habits you can develop.

Encouraging others also shapes you. It takes your focus off your own worries and reminds you that God is using you to build someone else up. It grows gratitude in your heart and creates stronger, healthier relationships. And best of all, it reflects God's heart—because He is the ultimate Encourager. When you lift others up, you reflect the hope, kindness, and strength of Jesus.

Reflection Questions:

1. Who in your life could use encouragement right now?
2. What holds you back from speaking words of life to others?
3. How has someone's encouragement helped you grow in the past?

Challenge for the Week: Encourage at least one person each day this week. It could be a kind message, a compliment, or simply telling someone they matter. Don't wait—your words could change someone's day.

Closing Prayer: *Lord, thank You for the people who've encouraged me. Help me be that kind of person for others. Show me who needs to hear a kind word, and give me the courage to speak life. Let my words reflect Your love. Amen.*

WEEK 36
LEADING BY EXAMPLE

START DATE: _____

Bible Verse: *"Set an example for the believers in speech, in conduct, in love, in faith and in purity."* — 1 Timothy 4:12b (NIV)

Devotional Message:

Leadership isn't just about having a title or being in charge. Some of the most powerful leaders are the ones who lead quietly—by living with integrity, kindness, and courage. You don't have to be the loudest voice to be the strongest example.

Paul encouraged a young Timothy, reminding him that age doesn't disqualify someone from making a meaningful impact. Instead of waiting for a future season, Timothy was challenged to lead through his everyday life—his words, his choices, his love, his faith, and how he carried himself. That's real leadership—the kind that doesn't demand attention but earns respect. God doesn't wait until you're older to use you. He invites you to lead right now, right where you are.

Whether you realize it or not, people are watching you. A younger sibling, a classmate, a teammate, or even a friend may look to you to see how a Christian lives. Your choices, your words, and your attitude send a message. What kind of message are you sending? Every decision—big or small—can be part of how you influence someone else's walk with God.

Jesus didn't lead with popularity or pressure. He led through compassion, truth, and humility. He served others, taught patiently, forgave freely, and modeled obedience to God. That's the kind of leader worth following—and the kind we're called to be.

So what does that look like in your life? It means speaking with kindness and respect, even when others don't. It means acting with honesty and staying true to your values, whether people are watching or not. It means loving others with compassion, staying rooted in God's truth, and living in a way that honors Him—heart, mind, and body. Choosing integrity when it's hard and leading with love when it's easier to judge may not always feel bold, but it's incredibly powerful.

You don't need a platform to make an impact. Quiet leadership through your daily choices often says more than any big speech ever could. And your faithfulness can spark something in someone else—the courage to follow God more closely.

Your example matters. You never know who you're inspiring just by living with purpose.

Reflection Questions:

1. Who is someone in your life that leads by example? What makes them stand out?
2. In what area do you want to be a better example to others?
3. How can you lead quietly this week through your choices and attitude?

Challenge for the Week: Choose one area—speech, conduct, love, faith, or purity—and focus on leading by example this week. Ask God to help you shine His light in small, daily moments.

Closing Prayer: *Lord, thank You for the opportunity to lead by example. Help me to reflect You in the way I live, speak, and love. Give me strength to stand out for the right reasons and the humility to lead in quiet, powerful ways. Amen.*

PART FOUR
PURPOSE, GOALS & LIVING OUT FAITH

WEEK 37

DISCOVERING YOUR PURPOSE

START DATE: _____

Bible Verse: *"For we are God's handiwork, created in Christ Jesus to do good works, which God prepared in advance for us to do."* — Ephesians 2:10 (NIV)

Devotional Message:

Have you ever looked in the mirror and wondered, *Why did God make me like this? What am I even here for?* It's a question that can sneak into your heart, especially when life feels ordinary, confusing, or like everyone else has it figured out. But here's the truth: you were intentionally made by the Creator of the universe. You are not random. God formed you with care, and He's already written good things into your story—even if you can't see them yet. *You were born on purpose, for a purpose, and not a single detail about you is an accident.*

Think of Esther, a young girl who probably never imagined she'd one day become queen and save her people. Yet when the moment came, she stepped into her purpose with courage and trust (Esther 4). Or think of David, the shepherd boy overlooked by everyone, but chosen by God to be king (1 Samuel 16). Neither of them saw the full picture of what God was doing—but they stayed faithful where they were. *Faithfulness in small things often opens the door to God's bigger plans.*

Your purpose isn't only about big achievements or someday dreams. It's about what you choose today. When you comfort a friend, help your sibling, speak kindly, or stand up for what's right —that's purpose in action. God can use even your everyday moments to shape your future and bless others.

Sometimes we believe purpose has to look big and dramatic—like solving world problems or becoming someone everyone knows. But God often works through what's quiet and unseen.

Jesus Himself spent most of His life not preaching to crowds, but living faithfully in a small town. When He began His ministry, He consistently noticed and cared for people others overlooked— because God's kind of greatness is rooted in love and humility.

If you don't know what your calling is yet, that's okay. You don't have to map out your whole future to be walking in purpose. Psalm 119:105 says God's Word is a lamp to our feet—not a spotlight to our future. He lights the way one step at a time.

So when you feel unsure or lost, remember this: God created you with a purpose that's unfolding day by day. You don't have to chase it—you just have to trust Him, follow Him, and let Him lead you into it.

Reflection Questions:

1. What do you feel passionate or curious about?
2. How are you using your time and gifts to honor God right now?
3. Are you willing to trust God with your future, even when it's unclear?

Challenge for the Week: Ask God to show you one small way to live out your purpose this week. Then do it—with joy and trust.

Closing Prayer: *Lord, thank You for creating me with purpose. Help me to trust Your plan, even when I don't see the whole picture. Show me how to live faithfully right now, and guide me toward the good works You've prepared for me. Amen.*

WEEK 38

USING YOUR GIFTS & TALENTS

START DATE: _____

Bible Verse: *"Each of you should use whatever gift you have received to serve others, as faithful stewards of God's grace in its various forms."* — 1 Peter 4:10 (NIV)

Devotional Message:

Have you ever noticed how certain things come easily to you—like writing, encouraging friends, solving problems, or making people laugh? Those aren't just quirks or coincidences. They're gifts, hand-picked by God and woven into who you are.

You were created with talents that reflect a small part of His heart, and they're meant to be used for something more than just your own enjoyment. *They're part of how you shine His light in the world, one moment at a time.*

God designed each of us with unique strengths so we could make a difference in the lives of others. In the early church, we see how God used all kinds of people to build His kingdom. Peter had boldness, John had deep compassion, and Lydia was known for her hospitality (Acts 16). They didn't all serve in the same way, but each one was important. The same is true for you—your gifts matter, and they're needed.

It can be easy to slip into comparison, especially when someone else's talents seem more exciting or popular. But God didn't create you to be a copy of anyone else. Instead of asking, "Why can't I be more like her?" try asking, "How can I use what God's given me?" *Comparison will always steal your joy, but gratitude for your unique strengths will help you grow.*

Using your gifts starts with paying attention to what comes naturally—and what brings you joy. Maybe you're a great listener, or maybe you love organizing things. Maybe you feel most alive when you're on stage, or maybe your strength is helping behind the scenes. Whatever it is, your gift isn't less valuable because it looks different from someone else's.

The next step is offering it back to God. Talent without purpose can end up feeling empty, but when you use your strengths to serve others, you'll find deeper meaning. Whether you're leading, creating, helping, or encouraging, your gifts can become a way to reflect God's love.

You don't need a huge platform or perfect skills to make a difference. You just need a willing heart. Start small. Be faithful. Look for one way this week to bless someone else with something God's given you.

Because your gift isn't just about what you can do—it's about who you're becoming as you use it for Him.

Reflection Questions:

1. What are some gifts or talents God has given you?
2. Are you using them to serve others, or mostly for yourself?
3. How can you grow in using your gifts for God's glory?

Challenge for the Week: Identify one gift you have and use it to bless someone else this week. Whether it's helping, encouraging, creating, or leading—do it with love.

Closing Prayer: *God, thank You for the gifts You've given me. Help me to see them clearly and to use them well. Show me where I can serve and how I can bring You glory with the talents You've placed in me. Amen.*

WEEK 39

HANDLING DISAPPOINTMENT WITH GRACE

START DATE: _____

Bible Verse: *"The Lord is close to the brokenhearted and saves those who are crushed in spirit."* — Psalm 34:18 (NIV)

Devotional Message:

Disappointment hits hard. Maybe you didn't make the team, your plans fell through, someone let you down, or life just didn't turn out the way you hoped. In those moments, it's easy to feel forgotten or frustrated with God. But disappointment doesn't mean God has abandoned you. It's actually where His grace often meets you most powerfully. *When your heart aches, He leans in — not away.*

God doesn't run from your disappointment—He draws near in it. He cares about your hurts, your setbacks, and the things that don't make sense right now. Even Jesus experienced disappointment. He was betrayed by a friend, rejected by His own people, and misunderstood by the very ones He came to save (John 1, Luke 22). Yet He faced it all with trust in God's plan and a heart full of grace. If the Son of God wasn't exempt from pain, we shouldn't be surprised when it finds us too—but we can be confident that God walks with us through it. *His love is steady, even when life feels unstable.*

So how can you handle disappointment with grace instead of anger, bitterness, or giving up?

• Be honest with God. Tell Him how you feel. He can handle your questions, tears, and frustration.

• Remember His promises. Just because this didn't work out doesn't mean He doesn't have something better ahead.

• Don't let failure define you. Disappointment isn't the end—it's often a setup for growth or redirection.

• Keep trusting. God's timing is different from ours, but it's always perfect.

Sometimes we're disappointed because we expected God to work a certain way—but He had a different plan. Looking back, you'll often see that what felt like a setback was actually protection or preparation.

His "no" or "not yet" is never the end of the story. And even when you don't get clear answers, God's presence is a promise you can count on.

Grace in disappointment means choosing trust over resentment. It means refusing to let one moment of pain steal your hope. And it means believing that God is still good, even when life doesn't go the way you wanted.

Reflection Questions:

1. What's one recent disappointment you've faced?
2. How did you respond, and what could you do differently next time?
3. What truth about God can you hold onto when life doesn't go as planned?

Challenge for the Week: Think of a disappointment you're still holding onto. Pray about it, then write down one positive lesson or shift in perspective that came from it—or could come from it.

Closing Prayer: *Lord, thank You for staying close when I feel disappointed. Help me to trust You, even when life doesn't turn out the way I hoped. Give me the grace to move forward in faith and to believe that Your plans are still good. Amen.*

WEEK 40

DREAMING BIG WITH GOD

START DATE: _____

Bible Verse: *"Now to him who is able to do immeasurably more than all we ask or imagine, according to his power that is at work within us."* — Ephesians 3:20 (NIV)

Devotional Message:

What are your biggest dreams? Maybe it's starting a business, becoming an artist, playing something professionally, traveling the world, or helping people in need. Dreams are exciting, and they're part of how God designed you. But the best dreams are the ones we build with Him.

Sometimes our dreams feel too big, too unrealistic, or too far away. But nothing you hope for surprises God. In fact, He often dreams even bigger than we do—and He has the power to bring those dreams to life in ways we can't always see from the start. *He sees not just where you are, but where He's taking you. And every step matters in His plan.*

God gave Joseph a dream when he was young (Genesis 37), but it took years—and a lot of setbacks—before that dream became reality. Along the way, he was sold into slavery, thrown into prison, and forgotten by people he helped. Yet in all of it, God was working. He used those hard seasons to shape Joseph's heart, build his faith, and prepare him for leadership. Your dream might take time too, but if it's from God, He'll carry it to completion in His perfect timing.

Dreaming big with God begins by inviting Him into your imagination.

Talk to Him about your hopes, and ask Him to shape your desires into something meaningful. Stay grounded in Scripture, because dreams that align with God's truth always have a stronger foundation. And don't be afraid of the growing process. Often, the challenges along the way are what strengthen your character and prepare you for what's ahead.

You don't need to wait until everything lines up perfectly before you take a step. Small acts of obedience matter. God often reveals the path one step at a time, and your willingness to move forward—even with uncertainty—is an act of trust. And if the dream shifts along the way, that's okay too. Sometimes God refines the dream as He refines you.

Dreaming big doesn't mean chasing fame, applause, or perfection. It means believing that your life has meaning and trusting that God can do more through you than you ever imagined.

You were created to live with purpose, to pursue bold, God-shaped dreams, and to trust the One who sees the full picture from the very beginning.

Reflection Questions:

1. What's one big dream God has placed on your heart?
2. How can you invite Him into that dream?
3. What's one step you can take this week toward that dream?

Challenge for the Week: Write down one dream you believe God has placed on your heart. Pray over it daily and take one small action toward it—no matter how simple.

Closing Prayer: *Lord, thank You for creating me with purpose and imagination. Help me to dream big—not for my own glory, but for Yours. Show me what You want to do through my life, and give me the faith to follow where You lead. Amen.*

WEEK 41

WHY EFFORT MATTERS

START DATE: _____

Bible Verse: *"Whatever you do, work at it with all your heart, as working for the Lord, not for human masters."* — Colossians 3:23 (NIV)

Devotional Message:

Have you ever tried your best at something—school, sports, a friendship—only to feel like no one noticed or that it still wasn't enough?

It's discouraging when your hard work doesn't lead to the recognition or results you hoped for. But here's the truth: in God's eyes, your effort always matters.

Colossians 3:23 reminds us to work at everything with all our hearts, not for human praise but for the Lord. That means your motivation shouldn't come from trying to impress people or win approval. Whether or not anyone else sees it, God does. And He values the heart behind what you do.

God isn't just measuring your success by the outcomes. He's looking at your faithfulness and your willingness to show up even when it's hard. When you study for a test, help your family, or encourage a friend, the way you do it—with love and care—matters deeply to Him.

Think about the widow in Luke 21. She gave only two small coins—barely anything compared to what others were giving—but Jesus said she gave more than anyone else. Why? Because she gave from the heart, out of trust and love for God.

Your quiet efforts, even when they feel small or unnoticed, can carry deep spiritual significance.

Giving your best doesn't mean being perfect. God isn't asking you to perform flawlessly—He's asking you to be faithful. He's forming your character through the process, building qualities like perseverance and discipline.

Sometimes, the most meaningful victories are the ones that no one else sees but God.

When you start to feel overlooked, shift your perspective. Ask yourself, "Am I doing this with a heart that honors God?" Even the smallest tasks—making your bed, showing up on time, putting in steady effort—can become acts of worship. *Faithfulness in the hidden places prepares you for impact in the visible ones.*

You may not always get recognition, and you may not always feel successful. But when you give your best for God, you're planting seeds of faith and strength that He will grow in His perfect time.

Reflection Questions:

1. Is there something in your life where you've felt discouraged despite your effort?
2. How can you shift your mindset to focus on working for God instead of people?
3. What's one area where you want to give your best this week?

Challenge for the Week: Pick one task—big or small—and commit to doing it with your whole heart this week, as if it's for God alone.

Closing Prayer: *Lord, thank You for reminding me that effort matters. Help me to work with a heart that honors You, even when no one else sees. Teach me to be faithful in the small things and to trust You with the results. Amen.*

WEEK 42

MONEY, SUCCESS & GOD'S PERSPECTIVE

START DATE: _____

Bible Verse: *"For where your treasure is, there your heart will be also."*
— Matthew 6:21 (NIV)

Devotional Message:

Money, popularity, and achievement aren't bad things. In fact, they can be amazing tools when used with wisdom and purpose. But when those things become what we chase most, they can quietly take over our hearts. Before we know it, we're measuring our worth by numbers—likes, grades, dollars, or compliments—and feeling empty when we don't measure up.

The things you value most will shape your thoughts, your decisions, and your identity. If your mind is always focused on image, approval, or material things, it's easy to feel anxious and never enough. But when your heart is centered on God, you begin to experience a steadiness that doesn't depend on status or success. *Peace grows when your priorities are rooted in something unshakable.*

Our culture constantly tells you that success means more—more attention, more beauty, more awards. But God defines success differently. In His eyes, success is about character. It's about how you treat people, how you trust Him when things are unclear, and how you honor Him in both the big moments and the quiet ones.

True success isn't about what you build, but about who you become while building it.

Solomon learned this the hard way. He had it all—wealth, wisdom, fame—but later realized that none of it satisfied his soul without a relationship with God (Ecclesiastes 1). His story reminds us that even the best accomplishments will feel meaningless if God isn't at the center of our lives.

So how do you keep your heart aligned with what matters most? Start with gratitude. When you focus on what you already have, it becomes easier to let go of comparison. Practice giving—your time, your gifts, or even your resources. Generosity shifts your focus from self to others. And most importantly, invite God into your dreams and goals. Ask Him to shape your definition of success so it reflects His heart, not just the world's expectations.

God isn't against ambition. He's the one who created you with talents and passions. But He wants your heart more than your accomplishments. When He's your treasure, everything else falls into place—and you'll find a kind of fulfillment that lasts far beyond any spotlight.

Reflection Questions:

1. What does success mean to you right now? Is it shaped more by the world or by God?
2. Do you ever feel pressure to "have more" or "be more"? Where do you think that pressure comes from?
3. How can you keep your heart focused on what really matters?

Challenge for the Week: Pick one way to shift your focus this week —like giving to someone in need, limiting social media comparison, or writing a gratitude list.

Closing Prayer: *God, help me see money and success through Your eyes. Remind me that true worth isn't found in things, but in You. Teach me to trust You with my goals, and to live with a heart that honors You above all. Amen.*

WEEK 43

WHEN LIFE FEELS UNFAIR

START DATE: _____

Bible Verse: *"The Lord is a refuge for the oppressed, a stronghold in times of trouble."* — Psalm 9:9 (NIV)

Devotional Message:

Sometimes life just doesn't feel fair. You work hard but get overlooked. Someone breaks the rules and gets rewarded. People get hurt who didn't do anything wrong. When that happens, it's easy to feel frustrated, confused, or even abandoned by God.

But God sees it all.

He knows your heart, your pain, and every question you've been too afraid to say out loud. He isn't distant in the middle of injustice —He's near, offering comfort, protection, and peace. When everything around you feels uncertain, He becomes the place you can run to and rest. You don't have to pretend everything's okay—God meets you right where you are. And He promises to hold you, strengthen you, and walk with you through the pain. *His presence is steady, even when nothing else makes sense.*

Jesus understands what unfairness feels like better than anyone. He was perfect, yet He was betrayed, mocked, and killed. And still, He didn't fight for revenge or lash out in anger—He trusted His

Father's plan, even when it led to the cross. His response reminds us that justice doesn't always happen right away, but God is still working behind the scenes in powerful ways. *His silence was not weakness—it was trust.*

When you're hurting, don't keep it all bottled up. Bring it to God honestly. He can handle your anger, your tears, and your questions. You might not be able to change the situation, but you can choose how you respond—and that choice can shape your character. Choosing grace, truth, and integrity in an unfair moment is one of the strongest things you can do.

Sometimes God allows hard things not to harm you, but to grow you. He uses the injustice you face to build empathy, resilience, and a deeper faith. Even when the world around you doesn't feel just, you can hold onto the truth that God is—and He's not done writing the story.

You may not be able to make life fair, but you can be someone who reflects fairness, kindness, and strength. That kind of faithfulness speaks louder than you know—and it points others to the God who promises to make all things right in the end.

Reflection Questions:

1. Have you experienced a situation recently that felt unfair? How did it affect you?
2. What does it look like to trust God in a moment you don't understand?
3. How can you be a voice for fairness and kindness, even when life doesn't feel just?

Challenge for the Week: If something feels unfair this week, pause before reacting. Pray first, then choose to respond with honesty, grace, and trust in God's bigger picture.

Closing Prayer: *Lord, sometimes life doesn't feel fair, and I don't always understand why. But I know You are good, and You see what I'm going through. Help me trust You, even when things don't make sense. Be my strength and my refuge. Amen.*

WEEK 44
DEALING WITH STRESS & PRESSURE

START DATE: _____

Bible Verse: *"Come to me, all you who are weary and burdened, and I will give you rest."* — Matthew 11:28 (NIV)

Devotional Message:

Stress is real. Between school, friendships, family expectations, social media, and future plans, it's easy to feel like you're being pulled in every direction. Some days, there just doesn't seem to be enough time, energy, or peace to keep going. But in the middle of the chaos, God offers something the world can't: deep rest—not just for your body, but for your soul.

Jesus doesn't ask you to fix everything before coming to Him. He simply invites you. You don't have to be strong enough, organized enough, or "together" enough to receive His peace. When life feels like too much, you can lean on Him instead of trying to carry everything alone.

Stress and pressure show up in different ways. Maybe you're trying to meet everyone's expectations, worrying about grades, comparing yourself to others, or feeling like you'll never catch up. But God never called you to be perfect. He asks you to bring your worries to Him and trust that He's strong enough to carry what you can't.

Even Jesus experienced pressure. He was constantly surrounded by people, questioned by religious leaders, and misunderstood by His closest friends. But He regularly stepped away from the noise to pray and rest. If He made time for quiet moments with God, so should we.

Sometimes we think being busy proves we're doing something right. But busyness doesn't always mean purpose, and exhaustion isn't a requirement for being faithful. True rest isn't laziness—it's obedience. It's recognizing that God is in control, not you, and trusting Him to hold what you can't manage.

One of the most powerful things you can do when you're over-whelmed is to pause and pray. Even a few minutes of silence in God's presence can shift your whole perspective. Ask Him for peace, for clarity, and for the strength to focus on what truly matters.

Let go of the pressure to do it all. You were never meant to carry the world on your shoulders.

Stress will always try to creep in, but God's presence is steady. He may not take away every challenge, but He walks with you through them. You don't have to push through alone. You can rest in the arms of a Savior who sees you, knows you, and never lets you go.

Reflection Questions:

1. What's causing you the most stress right now?
2. How do you usually respond when you feel overwhelmed?
3. What can you do differently this week to turn to God first?

Challenge for the Week: Take 10 minutes each day to pause, unplug, and pray. Ask God to help you release your stress and renew your strength.

Closing Prayer: *God, when life feels heavy, remind me to come to You. Teach me to rest in Your presence instead of pushing through on my own. Help me to trust that You are in control, even when I feel overwhelmed. Thank You for being my peace. Amen.*

WEEK 45
WHAT IT MEANS TO LEAD

START DATE: _____

Bible Verse: *"Whoever wants to become great among you must be your servant."* — Matthew 20:26b (NIV)

Devotional Message:

When you think of a leader, you might picture someone standing on a stage, giving orders, or being the center of attention. But Jesus flipped that idea completely. In His kingdom, leadership isn't about power or popularity—it's about serving others with humility and love.

That's the opposite of what the world teaches. Culture often says leaders should be bold, dominant, and in control. But Jesus redefined greatness. He showed that the most impactful leaders are often the quiet ones—the ones who lift others up, not to be seen, but because they care.

He didn't just talk about servant leadership—He lived it. Though He was the Son of God, He washed His disciples' feet, cared for the sick, and welcomed people others rejected. His leadership wasn't about demanding attention—it was about offering compassion, truth, and strength through sacrifice. *His power was expressed through love, not control.*

You don't need a title to lead. You lead every time you choose kindness over cruelty, honesty over convenience, and humility over pride. You lead when you support someone who's struggling or set a quiet example others can follow.

Leadership also happens in everyday choices—being the first to forgive, the one who includes others, or the one who keeps going when things get hard. Sometimes it means doing the right thing when no one thanks you or standing up for what's right even if you stand alone. These moments matter more than you realize, because they show others who you follow and what you value.

It starts with character. Be dependable, respectful, and gentle, even when no one's watching. Look for chances to serve, especially when it's inconvenient. And stay humble enough to keep learning—because true leaders never stop growing.

God doesn't need flashy leaders—He uses faithful ones. Every quiet act of integrity is shaping you into someone He can use in powerful ways.

Your influence may be bigger than you think. Someone is always watching how you live—whether it's a younger sibling, a friend, or someone who's searching for hope. When you lead with love, you show the world what it looks like to follow Jesus.

Reflection Questions:

1. Who do you look up to as a godly leader? What makes their leadership meaningful?
2. What's one area of your life where you could step up and lead more intentionally?
3. How does serving others help you grow as a leader?

Challenge for the Week: Look for one way to lead by example this week. Serve someone quietly, show integrity in a tough situation, or offer support where it's needed most.

Closing Prayer: *Jesus, thank You for showing me that leadership is about love and service. Help me to lead with humility, courage, and kindness. Show me how to use my life to lift others up and point them to You. Amen.*

WEEK 46
STANDING FOR WHAT'S RIGHT

START DATE: _____

Bible Verse: *"Be on your guard; stand firm in the faith; be courageous; be strong."* — 1 Corinthians 16:13 (NIV)

Devotional Message:

There will be moments in life when doing the right thing isn't easy. Maybe everyone around you is going along with something you know is wrong. Maybe you feel pressure to stay silent when someone's being mistreated, or you're afraid of being judged for standing up for your beliefs.

But following Jesus means having the courage to stand—even when it's uncomfortable.

God never promised that doing the right thing would be popular or simple. But He does promise to be with you, to give you strength, and to honor your faithfulness when you choose His way over the world's. Your willingness to stand firm in hard moments becomes a powerful act of trust.

Jesus stood up for what was right every single time. He called out injustice, stood with the outcasts, and stayed true to His mission even when it led to the cross. He didn't seek approval from the crowds—He stayed focused on His Father's will. That same focus is available to you when you draw near to Him.

Standing up for what's right doesn't always mean being loud or dramatic. Often, it looks like quiet conviction. Choosing not to cheat when others do, refusing to join in gossip, or standing beside someone who feels alone can be incredibly brave. Sometimes, the strongest stand you can take is the quiet choice to walk in integrity when no one else is. It might feel lonely—but it's never wasted.

Start by knowing the truth. The more time you spend in God's Word, the clearer your convictions become. Then pray for courage. God never expects perfection, but He loves when you come to Him for strength. Not everyone will understand or support your stand, but your value isn't in their approval—it's in being faithful to the One who made you.

You can be bold and still be kind. That's the kind of leader Jesus was, and that's the kind of example He invites you to follow. When you stand for truth with love and grace, you shine His light in dark places.

And even if you're the only one standing, you're never standing alone—God is always right there with you.

Reflection Questions:

1. When have you felt pressure to stay silent or go along with something you knew wasn't right?
2. What helps you stay strong in those moments?
3. How can you be both courageous and kind when standing for truth?

Challenge for the Week: Look for one moment this week where you can take a stand—whether it's speaking up, walking away, or showing kindness when it's hard.

Closing Prayer: *Lord, help me to stand firm in my faith, even when it's difficult. Give me courage to speak truth, strength to say no, and a heart that honors You in all I do. Let my life reflect Your love and light. Amen.*

WEEK 47

SEEING THE LEAST, LOVING THE FORGOTTEN

START DATE: _____

Bible Verse: *"Truly I tell you, whatever you did for one of the least of these brothers and sisters of mine, you did for me."* — Matthew 25:40 (NIV)

Devotional Message:

Some needs are easy to see—someone drops their books, and you help. But other needs are quieter. The girl who always eats alone. The classmate who seems angry all the time. The neighbor who never talks much anymore. These people are often overlooked, but not by Jesus. He sees them clearly—and He calls us to do the same.

When you care for someone who's hurting, left out, or struggling, you're not just doing a good deed—you're loving Jesus Himself. That's how closely He identifies with the "least of these." The way you treat people who have nothing to offer in return says more about your faith than any Bible verse you quote.

Jesus constantly sought out the people others ignored—the sick, the poor, the outcasts, the rejected. He didn't just talk about love; He walked straight into the mess and stayed there. And He invites you to do the same. Loving people in need won't always be convenient, comfortable, or easy—but it will always be holy.

Serving the overlooked means showing up when it's awkward, inconvenient, or risky. It's offering a listening ear to someone who feels invisible. It's noticing the kid who's never picked first, or giving up your weekend to volunteer at a shelter. It might mean giving your time, your comfort, or even your reputation.

But it's worth it—because you're stepping into the kind of love that changes lives.

You don't have to fix everything. You just have to be willing to show up. Ask God to open your eyes to the needs around you. Be brave enough to step into someone else's pain. And remember, small acts done with great love carry eternal weight.

When you serve the least, you're not just doing charity—you're honoring Christ. You're saying, "I see you," to someone who's been overlooked.

And in a world that moves fast and forgets the vulnerable, that kind of love stands out as something truly powerful.

Reflection Questions:

1. Who around you might be hurting or in need—but hiding it well?
2. What's one way you can step out of your comfort zone to show compassion this week?
3. How does serving someone in need help you understand Jesus' heart more deeply?

Challenge for the Week: Choose one person you often overlook—at school, at home, or in your community—and take a step toward serving or encouraging them. Pray that God would show you how to love them well.

Closing Prayer: *Jesus, help me to see others the way You do. Open my heart to those who are hurting or overlooked, and give me the courage to respond with love. Let my life reflect Your compassion, even when it's inconvenient. Thank You for loving the least—and for teaching me to do the same. Amen.*

WEEK 48

CHOOSING KINDNESS DAILY

START DATE: _____

Bible Verse: *"Be kind and compassionate to one another, forgiving each other, just as in Christ God forgave you."* — Ephesians 4:32 (NIV)

Devotional Message:

Kindness might seem small, but it can make a huge difference. It can brighten someone's day, soften a hard heart, or remind someone they're not invisible. In a world full of pressure, comparison, and quick judgments, choosing kindness is one of the most powerful ways to reflect Jesus.

Kindness isn't just about being polite when it's easy. It's choosing love when it's inconvenient. It's speaking gently when you feel irritated, helping without being asked, and forgiving when holding a grudge would be easier. It's about responding to others with the same grace God has shown you—even when it's not deserved.

Jesus modeled this beautifully. He stopped to listen, reached out to the hurting, and gave His time to people everyone else ignored. His kindness flowed from compassion, not from how others treated Him. He didn't wait for perfect moments—He created them through everyday love.

So how do you live that out? Start by noticing the people around you. Ask God to help you see who needs encouragement, comfort, or even just a smile. Use your words to speak life, not criticism. Be patient—with others and with yourself. Choose kindness when no one is watching, because that's when it matters most.

You may never fully know the impact of your kindness, but God sees it all. Sometimes it's the smallest gestures—a compliment, a thoughtful text, a silent decision not to join in gossip—that have the biggest ripple effects. Kindness builds bridges. It opens hearts. And it often does more than we realize, both in others and in us.

When you choose kindness again and again, it shapes your character. It helps you grow into someone who looks more like Jesus—not just on the outside, but deep in your heart. And over time, the habit of kindness becomes part of who you are.

And don't forget to be kind to yourself. Speak to your heart the way you would speak to a friend. You're not expected to have it all together—but you are invited to walk in grace.

Kindness starts with willingness. God takes that and turns it into something beautiful.

Reflection Questions:

1. When have you experienced someone's kindness in a way that stuck with you?
2. Where do you struggle most to be kind—at home, at school, or with yourself?
3. How can you build a habit of kindness into your daily routine?

Challenge for the Week: Each day this week, do one intentional act of kindness—especially toward someone who might not expect it.

Closing Prayer: *Lord, thank You for showing me perfect kindness through Jesus. Help me to follow Your example and choose kindness in my words, thoughts, and actions. Let my life reflect Your heart in both big and small ways. Amen.*

WEEK 49

LEAVING A LEGACY OF FAITH

START DATE: _____

Bible Verse: *"Let your light shine before others, that they may see your good deeds and glorify your Father in heaven."* — Matthew 5:16 (NIV)

Devotional Message:

You might not feel like it now, but your life is leaving a mark. The way you treat others, the choices you make, how you live out your faith—all of it is building a legacy. The question isn't whether you'll leave one. It's what kind of legacy you want to leave behind.

A legacy of faith doesn't come from being perfect or popular. It comes from being faithful in the little things—choosing kindness when it's easier to snap, holding onto your values when others compromise, and trusting God even when things don't make sense. Those everyday decisions might seem small, but they're shaping the story others will remember. Legacy isn't always loud—it's often built in silence, through steady choices that honor God when no one's watching.

Think about the people who've impacted your faith journey. It probably wasn't because they had it all together. It was their quiet strength, the way they loved people well, and how they made God feel real just by how they lived. Their legacy was built one day at a time—ordinary moments lived with extraordinary faith.

You have that same opportunity. Someone is watching your example, whether you realize it or not. A younger sibling, a classmate, a friend who's unsure about God—they're noticing how you handle pressure, how you treat people, and how you respond when life gets hard.

You may be planting seeds of faith in someone else just by staying faithful in your own walk. Even small, unseen moments of integrity can ripple into someone else's breakthrough.

So how do you build that kind of legacy? Stay grounded in God's truth. Let your daily choices reflect who you are in Christ, not just who you feel like being. Speak encouragement. Offer forgiveness. Stay faithful, even when you don't see immediate results. Be someone who builds others up rather than tears them down.

And remember—your struggles aren't wasted. God can use even your hardest seasons to help someone else feel less alone.

You don't have to wait until you're older or have it all figured out. You're shaping your legacy right now. One prayer, one act of courage, one quiet moment of faithfulness at a time.

Your life matters—and God is using it in ways you can't yet see.

Reflection Questions:

1. Who in your life has left a legacy of faith? What made their impact so lasting?
2. What do you want people to remember about how you lived your faith?
3. What small choices can you make today that build a meaningful legacy tomorrow?

Challenge for the Week: Write down one sentence that describes the kind of legacy you want to leave. Then ask God to help you live it out, one step at a time.

Closing Prayer: *God, help me live a life that points others to You. Let my words, actions, and heart leave a legacy of faith, love, and trust in Your promises. Use my life—even the small moments—for something lasting. Amen.*

WEEK 50

THE POWER OF GRATITUDE

START DATE: _____

Bible Verse: *"Give thanks in all circumstances; for this is God's will for you in Christ Jesus."* — 1 Thessalonians 5:18 (NIV)

Devotional Message:

Gratitude is powerful. It can shift your mood, soften your heart, and help you see God's hand even when life feels overwhelming.

But let's be honest—it's easy to be thankful when things are going your way. It's a lot harder when things are stressful, disappointing, or just plain unfair.

That's what makes true gratitude such a bold act of faith. God invites us to give thanks not just when life feels good, but even when it doesn't. Gratitude doesn't mean pretending everything's perfect—it means choosing to look for God's presence even in the middle of pain or waiting. It's not about ignoring the hard things— it's about refusing to let them steal your view of God's goodness.

Jesus modeled this beautifully. He gave thanks before feeding thousands, before raising Lazarus, and even during the Last Supper. His gratitude wasn't based on comfort—it was rooted in trust. That's the kind of gratitude we're called to grow into. And it starts with small choices made every day.

Gratitude keeps us from becoming bitter, jealous, or entitled. It reminds us that everything we have is a gift—our breath, our friendships, our salvation. When we thank God for what we do have, our focus shifts away from what we lack. *It realigns our hearts with what's eternal, not just what's temporary.*

So how do you actually live this out? Start by noticing the little things—a warm drink, a smile from a friend, a quiet moment at the end of a long day. Try keeping a gratitude journal and writing down three things you're thankful for each day. Speak your thanks out loud—to God, to the people around you, even to yourself. *The more you practice gratitude, the more naturally it will flow—especially when you need it most.*

When life gets hard, ask God to give you new eyes. Instead of asking, "Why is this happening?" try asking, "What are You teaching me through this?" Gratitude won't erase your struggles, but it helps you walk through them with a heart anchored in peace.

Worry shrinks. Comparison fades. And joy becomes easier to find. Gratitude opens your eyes to God's goodness—no matter what season you're in.

Reflection Questions:

1. What are three things you're thankful for today?
2. When have you seen God's faithfulness even during a hard time?
3. How can you practice gratitude when life doesn't go as planned?

Challenge for the Week: Write down three things you're thankful for each day this week. At the end of the week, look back and thank God for how He's shown up—even in the small moments.

Closing Prayer: *God, thank You for every good thing You've placed in my life. Help me to see Your blessings clearly, even on the hard days. Grow in me a heart of gratitude that doesn't depend on circumstances, but on who You are. Amen.*

WEEK 51

LIVING WITH INTENTIONALITY

START DATE: _____

Bible Verse: *"Teach us to number our days, that we may gain a heart of wisdom."* — Psalm 90:12 (NIV)

Devotional Message:

Life moves fast—school, activities, friendships, social media, goals, and distractions constantly pull you in different directions. It's easy to get caught up in doing without stopping to ask why.

That's why intentional living matters. It's about making choices on purpose, not just following the crowd or your impulses.

The Bible reminds us that our days are limited—and because of that, they're precious. God calls us to live each day with purpose, rooted in wisdom and guided by His truth. When you understand that time is a gift, you start treating your decisions, words, and habits with more care. Each day becomes a chance to live with purpose instead of just getting through it. Even your quietest days hold the potential to shape your future and someone else's. *You don't have to do something big to live with meaning—just something intentional.*

Intentional living doesn't mean having everything figured out. It means pausing to ask questions like: Does this choice reflect who I want to be? Is this helping me grow closer to God? Am I making time for what truly matters? These small moments of reflection can shape your entire direction.

Jesus lived with deep intentionality. He didn't rush from task to task —He made time for people. He paused to rest and pray. He knew His mission, and even in ordinary moments, He walked with purpose. His life shows us that meaning isn't found in busyness but in faithfulness.

You can begin living intentionally by starting your day with God, even if it's just a short prayer or verse. Let your values—like faith, kindness, and integrity—guide your decisions. Not every opportunity deserves a yes; sometimes, wisdom means saying no.

At the end of the day or week, take a moment to reflect. Were your words, actions, and time spent in a way that honored God?

Intentional living isn't about being perfect—it's about being present. It's about noticing your life, seeking wisdom, and choosing growth.

When you live with intention, even ordinary days can become meaningful and full of purpose.

Reflection Questions:

1. What are some areas in your life where you tend to act without thinking?
2. What would it look like to be more intentional in your faith, friendships, or habits?
3. What's one small change you can make to live with more purpose this week?

Challenge for the Week: Each morning this week, ask God to help you live intentionally. Choose one area—your time, your words, or your actions—and commit to being more mindful in it.

Closing Prayer: *Lord, teach me to live each day with purpose. Help me to focus on what matters and to align my choices with Your truth. Fill me with wisdom and guide my steps as I grow into the person You created me to be. Amen.*

WEEK 52

MOVING FORWARD IN FAITH

START DATE: _____

Bible Verse: *"Trust in the Lord with all your heart and lean not on your own understanding; in all your ways submit to him, and he will make your paths straight."* — Proverbs 3:5–6 (NIV)

Devotional Message:

You've made it—52 weeks of seeking God, learning truth, and growing in faith. That's an incredible accomplishment, and it's something to be truly proud of.

But here's the good news: this isn't the end. It's just the beginning. Everything you've learned has been preparing you for what comes next.

As life continues, you'll face new seasons, fresh challenges, and unexpected changes. You won't always know what to do, and sometimes the future may feel unclear, overwhelming, or even a little scary. But no matter what comes, you don't walk into it alone. When your heart leans fully on God rather than your own understanding, you open the door for Him to lead you step by step.

Moving forward in faith doesn't mean pretending everything is perfect or acting like you'll never struggle again. It means choosing to walk closely with God daily, especially when the path isn't obvious. The same God who walked with you through the past 52 weeks is already ahead of you, ready to lead you into what's next.

Jesus didn't just invite His disciples to believe from a distance—He called them to follow. To trust. To act. Faith was never meant to be passive. It's not just about what you know—it's about how you live out what you've learned. Real faith shows up in the way you make decisions, love people, and stay close to God through both the highs and the lows.

So as you move into the next chapter of your journey, keep God at the center. Start and end your days with Him. Stay faithful in the small, quiet choices that shape your character more than you realize. When He nudges your heart, don't be afraid to obey—even if it feels uncertain or scary. Let your life be built around the One who never changes, even when everything else does.

Surround yourself with people who strengthen your faith, cheer you on, and remind you of who you are in Christ. You were created on purpose, for a purpose that only you can live out. You have gifts to use, people to bless, and a story that God is still writing in beautiful ways.

You don't have to have everything figured out. You just have to trust the One who does.

Reflection Questions:

1. What have you learned about God this year?
2. How have you grown in your faith and character?
3. What next step do you feel God calling you to take in this season?

Challenge for the Week: Write a letter to your future self, reminding yourself of what God has done this year and what kind of faith-filled girl you want to keep becoming.

Closing Prayer: *God, thank You for guiding me through this year. Help me carry everything I've learned forward. Give me courage to trust You with every step, and faith to follow You wherever You lead. Amen.*

MOVING FORWARD

CONGRATULATIONS ON COMPLETING *Faith and Wisdom*!
You've spent 52 weeks seeking God, growing stronger in your faith, and learning how to live with confidence, grace, and purpose. That's a huge accomplishment—and it's just the beginning.

This isn't the end of your journey—it's the launchpad. Every verse you studied, every challenge you completed, and every prayer you whispered has helped build a foundation of wisdom and truth in your life. **You're not the same girl you were when you began**—and that's something worth celebrating.

Faith isn't just a quiet belief in your heart—it's the way you live, love, speak, and lead. Some days, walking with God will feel easy and joyful. Other days, it might feel uncertain or hard. But no matter what, you can trust that God is with you, guiding your steps and shaping your story with purpose.

Keep choosing to live with intention. Stay rooted in God's Word. Lean on prayer, especially when you feel overwhelmed. And don't be afraid to be the girl who shows kindness when it's not expected, who stands firm when it's not easy, and who shines light in places that feel dark.

You are wiser, stronger, and more equipped now than when you started—and that wisdom will keep growing as you walk with God.

Let compassion guide your friendships, courage lead your decisions, and truth anchor your heart. Be the kind of woman who lives boldly, forgives freely, and trusts deeply.

Most of all, remember this promise: *"She is clothed with strength and dignity; she can laugh at the days to come"* (Proverbs 31:25). You don't need to fear the future—you're walking into it hand-in-hand with the One who holds it.

God has begun a beautiful work in you—and He will be faithful to complete it. Keep showing up. Keep saying yes to Him. And keep living out your faith with wisdom, one day at a time.

Thank you for letting *Faith and Wisdom* be part of your journey. May your story continue to unfold with purpose, courage, and a deep, unshakable trust in the One who made you.

You are loved. You are called. You are ready.

Keep moving forward. 💜

DID YOU ENJOY THIS BOOK?

We hope this devotional has encouraged you to live boldly, love others, and grow stronger in your faith.

If you found this book was helpful…

🥯 **Please leave a Review**

Your review helps other guys like you find this book—and reminds them they're not alone on their journey. A sentence of two can make all the difference!

Scan or click the QR code below to leave a quick review.

If you would like to order another copy, just scan or click this:

Thank you for being part of something bigger. Keep showing up, standing strong, and living your faith out loud.

With love,

David & Mary Beth